The GameTracker™ Journal --
Scholastic Basketball Officiating Edition
is published by X60 MEDIA, LLC

This work refers to various copyrighted rules and regulations of official governing bodies for scholastic (NFHS) basketball. Please refer to the individual organization for detailed rule interpretations and guidelines. The publisher makes no representations, warranties, or implications as to accuracy of the information contained herein, as rules are updated periodically by their owners.

Individual trademarks are property of their respective owners.

© 2017 by X60 MEDIA, LLC

All rights reserved.
GameTracker™Journal and GREAT Official™are Official Trademarks of X60 Media, LLC

Created by Billy Martin, Tim Malloy and Al Battista

Additional resources and necessary corrections can be found at:

Ref60.com

First Printing: August 2017

Intro: Our Path Forward

Congratulations. By acquiring this book, you join the 24 million people that spend billions of dollars every year on self-improvement programs. This industry includes a variety of market segments from holistic institutes, infomercials, books and audio books, motivational speakers, websites, seminars, personal coaching, online education, weight loss, and stress management programs. This one if specifically for YOU -- the scholastic basketball referee!

Like all self-improvement programs, they come with a promise. So here's ours:

If you are diligent and follow this prescription for success... you will become a <u>better basketball official</u> by the end of <u>this season</u>.

In fact, you might even become (what we have determined to be) a GREAT Official™. That's right, great! More than just average. Better than just mediocre. We're talking GREAT. You will improve on a game-by-game basis by following some simple concepts, commit to on-going learning and applying some dedication to your personal journey this season.

It doesn't matter if you are months away from opening day or deep into the season ... it is never too early, or too late, to begin this path forward.

Tools for Improvement

This *GameTracker Journal* is a key tool in the GREAT Official™ framework that will guide you each and every game to be a better referee. It's up to YOU to make the commitment and trust the improvement process.

This tool is broken into three major components:

- This <u>Intro</u> section – <u>Our Path Forward</u>, will also give you an overview on HOW to use the GameTracker Journal, as a tool. Additionally in <u>Part 1</u> we will guide you on a key exercise in goal setting called <u>V2MOM</u> (pronounced Vee-Two-Mom). We recommend you read this carefully and complete the V2MOM activities that are designed to get you started on the right foot this season. There is a checklist on page 8 to guide you. This is your blueprint for success --- so follow it carefully!

- <u>Part 2</u> describes what a <u>GREAT Official</u>™ looks like. If you could be the model referee, what would that be? We have provided a comprehensive framework of the key competencies you should aim for when developing as an official. Use this model as a foundation for setting your personal improvement goals this coming season.

- The final section <u>Part 3</u> and back-half of this tool is the actual <u>GameTracker</u>™ <u>Journal</u>. This is where you will live and breathe each and every game. We have provided 60 games worth of inspiration, learning and self-improvement tools. It is designed for you to capture feedback, assessments, ideas, notes and future improvement tasks as the season progresses.

How to Use This Journal

Here are some guidelines and suggestions to follow for getting the most out of this tool.

Break Your Status-Quo

Just like with starting a fitness regimen or new diet, the initial change might feel strange or even painful. However, the long-term benefits of sticking with a proven program certainly outweigh the short-term discomfort. This program is most likely different from your normal in-season routine. Use this opportunity to grow and break your personal status-quo and try a new approach to improving your refereeing ability. You will be happy with the results!

Develop Retention in Pieces (DRIP)

To foster ongoing learning and officiating development, your GameTracker™ Journal has 60 days (or games) worth of inspirational quotes, rules education and challenge questions. You will find these on the LEFT HAND SIDE pages of the tracker.

Here you are presented with a scholastic (NFHS) basketball officiating rule topic along with an associated quiz question each day. The answers to each Challenge question can be found on the following day page.

Hopefully, continued education is one of your personal goals for this year. Use the GREAT Official™ tools to spark learning and identify gaps in your knowledge of the rules.

Get the Pencil Ready

Well, maybe a pen! Yes, this is not only a journal but a workbook and game tracker, all-in-one. That means it is all about writing and documenting on a consistent basis various items that will improve your officiating performance. If you are not the type of person who likes writing things down, our suggestion is to try it for 30 straight days without interruption. Most habits can be created by continuing something for a solid month or more. This journal will provide a framework and toolset to capture pregame and postgame analysis of you and your crew.

Pregame Planning

If you follow this prescriptive plan, pregame preparation is another image of difference.

Your personal journal asks some key questions for every game. While much of this information might be found in your online scheduling system (i.e. The Arbiter, etc.) there is one critical question that you should commit to answering EVERY GAME. This is committing to ONE THING you will do different every game... and writing it down ahead of time. Leverage the pregame planning component of your GameTracker™ to capture these actionable goals.

Postgame Assessment

Just as important as all your learning and preparation prior to your season is getting in the routine of a real honest and open dialogue with your crew AND with yourself regarding your performance. This should be a fully transparent conversation immediately after the game while still in the locker room <u>BEFORE</u> you leave the facility.

It's certainly understood that many times you and your partner or crew might be leaving a school or rec center immediately after the game. While this may be the case, it is recommended to still follow this simple cadence of three questions. (see diagram)

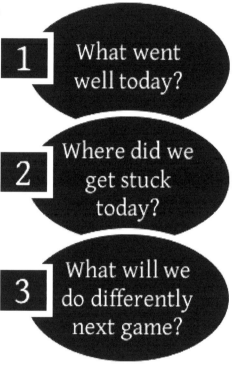

1 What went well today?

2 Where did we get stuck today?

3 What will we do differently next game?

Whether or not you are the crew chief, referee or lead official on the game does not matter. <u>YOU</u> can be the one to spark this discussion and ask these three simple questions.

Notice all of the questions are positive in nature. By not asking questions like, *"what did we do wrong?"* or *"where did we mess up out there?"* is important. By soliciting and sharing positive feedback as the crew, this sets the stage for a thorough postgame assessment.

Always allow your partner/crew to respond to these questions first and then provide your feedback. Have the GameTracker™ Journal out and record this feedback. This will help you build on the positives, remove obstacles and identify areas of improvement for the future as an individual and as a crew.

<u>Officiating Performance Assessment</u>

This journal includes an area for personal or a crew's assessment of on-court performance for up to <u>60 GAMES</u> in a season.

YOUR PERFORMANCE ASSESSMENT					
Decision Accuracy	1	2	3	4	5
Rules Knowledge	1	2	3	4	5
Floor Mechanics	1	2	3	4	5
Game Management	1	2	3	4	5

<u>Note</u>: Please refer to the GREAT Official™ section of this journal for details on recommended performance assessment criteria.

The best part about this assessment scale (1 through 5) is that <u>YOU OWN IT</u>. Typically 5 is excellent and 1 is poor but you can decide. The key is to be diligent and consistent in assessing your own performance each and every game <u>and</u> committing this to your journal in writing.

The actual numbers are not as important as spotting trends in the categories. Are you consistently scoring yourself or your partner/crew extremely low in a certain area? Do you see a pattern that emerges throughout the season?

The GameTracker™ Journal is <u>YOUR</u> tool to make out of it what you want. This can be an extremely valuable component of your officiating growth <u>or</u> it might not be "your style" to track your career is such a way. Regardless, of your method, the building blocks of learning, preparation and assessment are the foundation that supports continuous growth and will help every official reach their career goals.

<u>Notes</u>

Getting Started Checklist

Follow this checklist to start your journey to becoming a GREAT Official™. Do not skip any parts as there is no shortcut on the path to success. So let's get started.

❏ ## Read the "Our Path Forward" Intro Section

If you have been reading along to this point, it is all good. If not, go back and read the "Our Path Forward" section to make sure you are well-grounded and ready to start. This section also contains tips and tricks to leverage the GameTracker™ during your season.

❏ ## Part 1: Create Your Officiating V2MOM

Read the section on "The Keys to Success: Goal Setting & Focus" starting on page 10. Make sure to complete your personal V2MOM as the very first step in a professional improvement plan for this season. Remember, there is no shortcut to success!

❏ ## Part 2: Learn How To Be a GREAT Official™

The competencies and skills required to be not just good -- but great -- are included in this toolset. Use this model as a foundation for your game preparations and assessments throughout your season.

❏ ## Part 3: Commit To Your Daily GameTracker™

The image of difference here is all about continuous improvement from one game to the next. This game tracking tool provides you with a mechanism to be inspired, educated and challenged each and every day. Commit to the process and use the tools to gather and provide feedback to yourself and crew, each and every game.

<u>Notes</u>

Part

1

Creating Your

V2MOM

The Keys to Success: Goal Setting & Focus

We have all heard the saying, *"It's not a goal if it's not written down."* Well that is partially true. It is also not a goal if you cannot measure success when you have arrived at that goal.

There are perhaps thousands of goal-setting and management philosophies. All of these share striking similarities. Many of them are hard to understand let alone implement personally or for an organization. In search of an "easy to use" system to spark the software giant Salesforce (NYSE:CRM), founder and CEO Marc Benioff created his own management system to solve this challenge.

Salesforce, now almost 20 years old, implemented this approach from Day One for its employees. Today over 30,000 internal employees and dozens of other partner companies use this method to goal set and keep in alignment with those goals. Mr. Benioff calls it the V2MOM Method. (pronounced Vee-Two-Mom)

The V2MOM is a powerfully simple approach that allows individuals, even basketball officials, to clarify what they are doing to achieve a common goal. In the corporate world it is all about the company's success. In the officiating world, it is all about YOUR PERSONAL success and supporting the mission of your local officiating organization.

So let's get started and create YOUR V2MOM that will guide your journey this season!

What is Your Vision?

The very first component of creating your V2MOM is to think about your ultimate goal. Think about these simple questions before we commit your vision to paper.

- Where do you want to go as an official?
- What type of referee do you want to be?
- Where do you see yourself by the end of the season?
- What type of journey would you like to go on?
- What does <u>success</u> look like?

Do you want to move up to a different level of officiating? Are you a cadet-in-training and just want to be comfortable working your first season? Do you want to learn and be proficient in the 3 person mechanics system? Do you want to teach others how to be a great official as well?

What is <u>YOUR</u> vision for this year? It's all about you. The wording is not as important as the actual meaning and your understanding of your vision.

On the next page ... let's take a first whack at creating this vision.

Use this area to scratch notes and create a first version of your vision. Don't worry, it is just a rough draft. We will bring the final words into a complete V2MOM later in your journal.

So let's get visioning as the first step in creating your V2MOM!

Visioning Worksheets

Here is a real example that might spark your own personal vision.

My _VISION_ for this year is to be working a full varsity schedule by season's end. I will be confident in my rules Knowledge and aim to receive all positive feedback from my observers and coaches. I will mentor one young official this year as well.

Write Down Your Vision:

_____

_____

_____

_____

_____

_____

Share Your Values

Congrats on creating your Vision - which is the first "V" in this newly evolving personal V2MOM. *Remember it is pronounced Vee-Two-Mom!*

The "second V" in the V2MOM stands for Values.

Your Values should connect back to your Vision and answer a few simple questions:

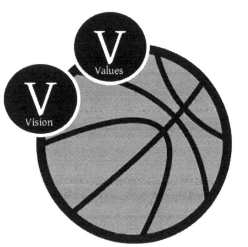

- What is so <u>important</u> about achieving this vision?
- What are your personal <u>principles</u> and <u>beliefs</u> that will guide you toward this vision?

A person's values, like a moral compass, should connect directly to your Vision and be prioritized in order of importance. What is MOST important to you? What do you value most?

Yes, these questions might leave you head-scratching, but that is a good thing. On the following pages, write down your thoughts on these personal principles and beliefs that will guide you toward success.

Here we go ... what are <u>YOUR</u> Values?

<u>Notes</u>

Values Worksheet

Let's build on the previous Vision example and share our Values:

My <u>VISION</u> for this year is to be working a full varsity schedule by season's end. I will be confident in my rules knowledge and aim to receive all positive feedback from my observers and coaches. I will mentor one young official this year as well.

I <u>VALUE</u> the following principles that will guide me to success this year.
- Learning Something New Every Game
- Being a Trustworthy Partner and Crew Member
- Friendships and Camaraderie
- Open to Critique on My Officiating Skills
- "Pay It Forward" through Mentoring

Write down your Values in order of importance:

_____

_____

_____

_____

_____

_____

_____

_____

_____

_____

Methods Are How You Get There

You have a great start on defining your visionary goals for the season and what you value along the way. Now it is time to think about <u>HOW</u> you will get there. This is the "M" in our V2MOM.

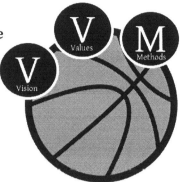

Methods are <u>specific and measurable</u> actions or tasks that you will execute on a daily, weekly and monthly basis to be successful as an official - and make your vision come true! This is your tactical plan.

Take special notice to the measurable component of a method. If you cannot measure your actions, then you never really know when the journey is successful.

These are the questions you should ask when crafting your V2MOM methods:

- Is this task <u>SPECIFIC</u> enough that anybody reading it would understand?
- Can the method be <u>MEASURED</u>? And how? We will address this at the end.
- Is the method <u>ACTIONABLE</u>? Is this dreaming or can you actually do what you say.
- How is the method <u>RELATED</u> to your goals and vision? It should be clear.
- Are the methods <u>TIME BOUND</u>? What's your cadence for doing it? How often or how much?

While many people think goal setting (Vision) and sharing your beliefs (Values) are somewhat "fluffy," the crafting of your Methods is much more concrete. These are the ACTUAL TASKS you will do on a regular cadence to reach your goal. Sounds simple, right? Creating these methods are much easier than staying on task with them.

Methods Worksheet

Let's see how our sample V2MOM is coming along and start to craft your own Methods for this season.

My _VISION_ for this year is to be working a full varsity schedule by season's end. I will be confident in my rules Knowledge and aim to receive all positive feedback from my observers and coaches. I will mentor one young official this year as well.

I _VALUE_ the following principles that will guide me to success this year.
- Learning Something New Every Game
- Being a Trustworthy Partner and Crew Member
- Friendships and Camaraderie
- Open to Critique on My Officiating Skills
- "Pay It Forward" through Mentoring

My METHODS for this Season:

1) Allocate two Sunday evenings to Rule and Case Book Review
2) Take the Pre-Season Review Test until I get a 90 percent grade.
3) Conduct (or Participate) in a Pregame Discussion for EVERY game.
4) Write a Journal Entry for Every Game in my GameTracker
5) Ask for and give feedback with 80+ percent of my games.
6) Connect with the cadet I'm mentoring weekly.
7) Attend the monthly basketball club meetings to meet new officials and coaches.

Write down your Methods and number them in order of importance:

Obstacles In The Way

Hopefully you were able to think about the tasks you will be able to execute throughout your busy season. Unless officiating is your only job, there will be a number of personal issues (i.e. work, family and social commitments, etc.) that must be accounted for and fit into your 24-hour day.

Now is a good time to revisit your VISION and assess if by doing a bang-up job on METHODS you can actually achieve your goals. Is it still realistic? Or is this an unrealistic wish that has little chance of success?

If you determine your goals and vision are still viable, then it is time to think about the interference that will stand in your way. The "O" in V2MOM stands for Obstacles.

While it is possible you cannot envision any obstacles blocking your way; it is more likely there are certain external factors that will be impediments along your journey.

Some key questions you should ask when identifying potential obstacles are:

- Is the obstacle a "show-stopper" or is it something that I can overcome?
- Do I have control of these obstacles, or not?
- Are there too many obstacles to consider that I cannot execute on my methods?

Obstacles should be directly related to your methods. Let's see how our sample V2MOM has identified some obstacles in the way of success, and start to craft your own.

Obstacles Worksheet

My <u>METHODS</u> for this Season:

1) Allocate two Sunday evenings to Rule and Case Book Review
2) Take the Pre-Season Review Test until I get a 90 percent grade.
3) Conduct (or Participate) in a Pregame Discussion for EVERY game.
4) Write a Journal Entry for Every Game in my GameTracker
5) Ask for and give feedback with 80+ percent of my games.
6) Connect with the cadet I'm mentoring weekly.
7) Attend the monthly basketball club meetings to meet new officials and coaches.

<u>OBSTACLES</u> that stand in my way:

- My partner likes to watch TV on Sunday Nights (might have to compromise)
- Test Review Groups meet on Tuesday and it makes a long day.
- Many times we arrive right before afternoon games and don't have time for a pre-game.
- Some senior officials don't like to give feedback (or take it)
- The club meetings are open to members only
- Office is busy and New Project is Time Consuming
- My ankle has been bothering me and I'm running slower

Write down the Obstacles you see standing in the way.
Later you might address these in your Methods to minimize their impact on your season.

Measuring Success

You are almost there.

The last stop of our V2MOM creation is "M" for Measures. It is all about knowing when you have arrived!

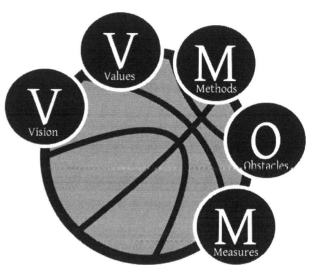

Did you actually "do" what you said you were going to do? Were you able to execute on the methods (tasks) as you originally planned? Did you accomplish your Vision and reach your goals?

Measures can be numbers or metrics. They can also be yes or no. Did you achieve this or not. Most importantly, all Measures are <u>TIED DIRECTLY</u> to <u>EACH ONE</u> of your Methods. If you have six Methods, then you should have one Measure for each - a total of six. A Method is not a Method if you cannot Measure it!

Measures Worksheet

Here's an example of the Measures tied to our sample V2MOM that will help you craft yours.

My METHODS and MEASURES for this Season:

1) Allocate two Sunday evenings to Rule and Case Book Review
<u>Measure</u>: Accomplished (Yes or No)

2) Take the Pre-Season Review Test until I get a 90 percent grade.
<u>Measure</u>: My Score is _ _ _ _ _

3) Conduct (or Participate) in a Pregame Discussion for EVERY game.
<u>Measure</u>: Number of PreGame Discussions = _ _ _ _ _ _

4) Write a Journal Entry for Every Game in my GameTracker
<u>Measure</u>: Completed (Yes or No)

5) Ask for and give feedback with 80+ percent of my games.
<u>Measure</u>: _ _ _ _ percent of games with feedback

6) Connect with the cadet I'm mentoring weekly.
<u>Measure</u>: Accomplished (Yes or No)

7) Attend the monthly basketball club meetings to meet new officials and coaches.
<u>Measure</u>: Accomplished (Yes or No) or _ _ _ _ _ Number Out of _ _ _ _ _

Look back at YOUR Methods and think about how you would Measure success for <u>each one</u>.

_____

_____

_____

_____

_____

_____

_____

_____

_____

_____

Pulling it All Together

Use the template that can be found in your GameTracker™ Journal to gather previous worksheet notes and create your <u>FINAL V2MOM</u>.

This will be your "North Star" and guide you to success this season. Setting your direction is an important step in becoming a GREAT Official™. Do not take short-cuts!

Part
2

The GREAT
Official™

How Good Can You Be?
The GREAT Official™ Competency Model

If you have been in the business of officiating for any length of time you likely have heard a variety of negative comments from fans, players and even coaches about your personal efforts on the court. It is part of the game that we must learn to deal with, but also learn to judiciously muster the courage to penalize this type of conduct when it becomes excessive or unsportsmanlike.

But how often do you hear the opposite? That he or she is a "great official." It is rare, but unsolicited compliments occasionally are offered to unsuspecting officials.

Most sports officials were trained with the goal of being invisible and unnoticed during the course of a game. By achieving this, from an outsider's perspective, they feel good about your on-court performance. However in reality, this well-intended goal misses the mark.

Being "great" is more than just going unnoticed in a game. It is about striving for a common set of knowledge and skills that over time have proven to be successful in our craft of sports officiating. When knowledge and skill are harnessed together, they drive behavior.

So what is a competency?

In the business world, a competency is a general description of requirements an employee must achieve to be successful in an organization. But in our world of sports, competencies are what officials need to be successful on the court. It is important not to confuse tasks with competencies. Competencies are much more comprehensive.

Competencies include related...

- Personal Attributes - your fitness, appearance and other factors.
- Knowledge - specific to rules and mechanics.
- Skills- the ability to translate knowledge into on-court performance.
- Abilities- your capacity to grow and improve as an official.

... that form the responsibilities of being a sports official. Let's see how they come together to make us a great official.

The GREAT Official™ Model

The three authors of this workbook have been fortunate and healthy enough to work for more than a combined total of 120+ years. And while we give thanks for the gift of longevity that allows us to continue in this great avocation, we have attempted to express our gratitude by sharing our collective experiences in this GameTracker™ Journal.

Note: On the Web, check out Ref60.com for more learning tools.

Addressing the challenges of assessing quality across an independent contracting organization, such as your local referee association, can be daunting. The Great Official's™ Model and the accompanying resources are a determined effort to arm YOU with the necessary tools to achieve mastery in this avocation.

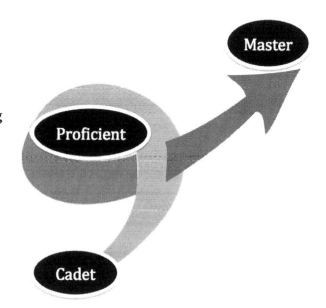

Know What Great Looks Like

It is why we have created this Great model. It answers the question, *"where should the bar be set?"*

Not everyone is committed to ongoing self improvement. Many officials become complacent and get lulled into a false sense of proficiency. And some folks are just in it for what the extra spending money can finance (i.e. holiday gifts; vacations; school tuitions, etc.) and not for the pure love of the game.

The tent of officiating takes in all kinds. But for the officials who make this model part of their personal improvement material, we promise you will be a better referee for it, and on your way to becoming a GREAT Official™!

And what does it take to to be a great official when you step on the court? The answer is... a never ending journey that requires continuous feedback, ongoing education and a constant sharpening of your skills.   While being proficient can be rewarding and provide stability; the great officials are entrusted with the higher level games that carry more fan interest and typically have more on the line.

Openly Assess Yourself

It is all about looking in the mirror. Understanding the man, or woman, in the glass

Keep in mind, assessing yourself goes far beyon the science of personality, and pivots toward several other key competency areas - including knowledge (the things you know); mechanics (the things you do); and judgement (how you apply everything to make snap decisions.)

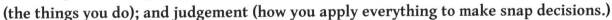

Decision Accuracy is the Ultimate Goal

When you put all these competencies and skills together, the ultimate goal is to make accurate decisions. It is that plain and simple. Decisions are judgments based on the current situation and the actual application of the proper rules. Like a judge in a courtroom -- sometimes you put the offenders in jail and other times the defendants (i.e. players and coaches) are exonerated without penalty. In a split second you are the judge and jury.

This means that not blowing your whistle is still a decision. Many decisions are judged on the legality of contact or a particular play by NOT blowing your whistle. A 'no call' in a contest can be as critical as the calls you make.

This balance of decision accuracy between rulings you make and others you pass on represent a qualitative aspect of officiating. While subjectivity is entered into the equation through careful scrutiny of game video or post-game debriefs with your crew - key decisions can be evaluated for correctness.

Following many of the collegiate and professional organizations that provide dedicated evaluation staff to assess this accuracy - the GREAT Official™ Model provides similar tools for the scholastic referee to assess your own decision accuracy. We call this the *Officiating Decision Tracker (ODT)* - and give you access to this tool and process to break down your games just like the professionals.

Even without using a tool like the ODT, you can assess yourself and partner/crew each and every game by looking at the accuracy of correct calls (and no calls) versus incorrect in a postgame discussion, or by reviewing the game video.

> <u>Note</u>: *Visit Ref60.com and search for "ODT" to download your complimentary PDF file of this Officiating Decision Tracker and more information on how to use it.*

Officiating Decision Tracker

Teams: _____ Level: _____ Date: _____

Crew: (R) _____ (U1) _____ (U2) _____

Quality Key: CC = Correct Call   CNC = Correct No Call   iC = Incorrect Call   INC = Incorrect No Call

Decision (Number)	Type (Violation Foul - Other?)	Call Quality (See Key)		Observation: Positioning / Mechanics / Rules (What was observed on court)	Focus of Improvement (What the crew / official can do better next time)
		CC	iC		
		CNC	INC		
		CC	iC		
		CNC	INC		
		CC	iC		
		CNC	INC		
		CC	iC		
		CNC	INC		
		CC	iC		
		CNC	INC		
		CC	iC		
		CNC	INC		
		CC	iC		
		CNC	INC		
		CC	iC		
		CNC	INC		
		CC	iC		
		CNC	INC		

Correct Calls _____   # Incorrect Calls _____

Correct No Calls _____   # Incorrect No Calls _____

Page _____ of _____

Rules Knowledge is Next

If you have read previous articles and books from "60 Seconds on Officiating" you might remember our position on what coaches can question you on.

There are three areas:

1) Integrity -- you should never put yourself in a position to be questioned on integrity.

2) Judgment -- occasionally, if done respectfully, you should be approachable to explain a judgment decision, in a professional and courteous way.

3) Rules Knowledge -- is something you <u>ALWAYS</u> should be prepared to be questioned on. Learning the rules and how to apply them is a foundational component of becoming a GREAT Official™.

You must master the rules before stepping on any court as a novice. But what about an experienced official? Are you spending the appropriate amount of time each year to, 'sharpen your sword?'

As part of our Ref60 (www.ref60.com) commitment to teaching, there are dozens of "paramedic training" articles, books and tools designed to prepare you for all the typical challenging rulings. Both IAABO and NFHS provide dozens of great tools to help you master this part of the game. It is up to you to take advantage of these.

Game Management is Dead Center

When it comes to getting down to business, the best officials can manage ANY game situation. Sitting in a classroom can only do so much in preparing you to handle the rigors of a challenging scholastic contest.

Ironically, some of the key game management competencies have very little to do with the game itself. Items such as punctuality, professionalism, resolving conflict, and general situational awareness all play a major role in overseeing a game from tipoff to final buzzer. Some of this is inherent in our "officiating personality" and other areas can actually be learned.

Areas that are taught include pregame preparations (conferences), handling substitutions, dead ball efficiency and bench/fan decorum. Game management can be observed and measured yourself (via video recording) and by peers or supervisors. A good chunk of an official's review would include how well they manage the game.

Note: Check out Ref60.com for articles touching all the key components of game management and how they are observed using these assessment tools.

Proper Floor Mechanics for All

You likely have heard the saying, *"if you look good, you are good,"* and this axiom certainly holds true for officiating. But this goes deeper than just physical appearance, and includes your ability to move and position yourself to improve your calling accuracy.

While taking it to the extreme and being robotic as an official is not the goal; you must accept the fact that there is one set of mechanics to follow as a scholastic official, just as you work to enforce the o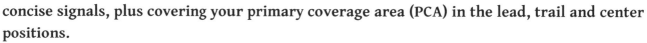 set of rules that govern the game.

This can be one of the more challenging aspects of the game to master as you try to blend your energy and personality into mechanics uniformity.

Assessing proper mechanics covers many different skills including proper use of the whistle, clear and concise signals, plus covering your primary coverage area (PCA) in the lead, trail and center positions.

Prescribed mechanics are rules of expression for referees. There are approved signals and a proper sequence of applying them in the ruling of a violation or foul, and you must work diligently to develop mechanics that allow you to confidently express yourself on the floor in a way that also conforms to the stated mechanics.

During a self-assessment or peer observation proper mechanics are easy to spot if you know what you are looking for - especially on video. You should consult your local or state organization for approved deviations from these typical NFHS and IAABO mechanics.

Comportment is the Final Piece

Comportment is the most subjective of all the key building blocks and is open to the most interpretation.

For our purposes, comportment is your behavior an demeanor as a sports official. For officials working game involving teams they have officiated before, your comportment is what coaches, players and fan remember when they see you walk in the door. And if it is the first encounter with a team, their opinior of your comportment will be what they form as you are heading to your car for the ride home.

Comportment is what makes you - you. Some factor are genetic and others acquired.

These include things like your physical appearance, fitness levels and other intangibles like body language, communication and approachability. In our GREAT Official™ model, we lump in officiating personality as "driver" of comportment.

Full details of the entire GREAT Official™ model is beyond the scope of this journal. Please visit Ref60.com for details, assessment criteria, exciting updates and more educational materials designed to make <u>YOU GREAT</u> in your officiating journey.

Notes

Part

3

GameTracker™

Journal

My Officiating V2MOM

My Vision

My Values

See Page 9 for More Information

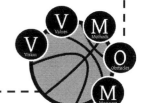

My Officiating V2MOM

My Methods & Measures

My Officiating V2MOM

Obstacles In My Way

Inspire

Optimism

"Write it on your heart that every day is the best day in the year."

No one in the history of sports officiating has ever been forced to be a referee. The task has never been part of a criminal sentence or a civil judgement, so there should not be the level of angst, stress and disappointment associated with the avocation.

Officiating is a privilege, not a punishment. You have requested to walk this path, and you have been given access to the journey. With this important attitude adjustment, every game will be more enjoyable.

Learn

Airborne Shooter

An airborne shooter is a player that has released the ball on a try for goal (or tapped the ball) and has not returned to the floor.

Protecting the airborne shooter is a key focus for your crew. This is accomplished by not turning your head too early when the shooter releases the ball --- and making sure they return to the floor safely and without being fouled.

Once the shooter releases the ball they are protected until at least one foot returns to the floor. If they are fouled (while airborne) after this release they are still considered to be "in the act of shooting."

Challenge

Q1: Airborne A-1 is fouled by B-1 before releasing the ball on a try for goal.
Is A-1 is considered an airborne shooter?

Y   N

Challenge Question answers can be found by turning the page each day.

Plan

PREGAME

Day / Date:

Location / Level / Tip Time:

Travel Time:

Leave By Time:

My Partner(s):

One thing I will try to do better in today's game is ...

Assess

POSTGAME

What went well today?

Where did we get stuck today?

What will we do different next game?

YOUR PERFORMANCE ASSESSMENT					
Decision Accuracy	1	2	3	4	5
Floor Mechanics	1	2	3	4	5
Game Management	1	2	3	4	5
Rules Knowledge	1	2	3	4	5
Comportment	1	2	3	4	5

☐ Pregame Conference Completed

☐ Postgame Review Completed

$ _____
Fee Amount

☐ Payment Received

Integrity

"If you don't stand for something you will fall for anything."

Ambition is a critical component for advancing your officiating career, but hopefully your core values are anchored on moral high ground and they can be easily integrated into your avocation.

Being an official with integrity means that you never stand on the neck of another official to raise your own profile. And you remember to treat with respect and honesty, the assignors at each level who gave you your early breaks. Don't thoughtlessly cast them aside as merely pawns to use for your advancement.

Team-Control

While the ball remains live, a loose ball always remains in control of the team whose PLAYER had control, unless it's a try or tap for goal.

Understanding the concept of "control" is a basic fundamental of officiating. Whenever a player has control - their team is also considered to be in control. This includes while the ball is being passed among teammates or even when a player's dribble is temporarily interrupted.

There is NO team-control while the ball is in flight for a try (or tap) for goal, during rebounding action or a jump ball. If a player on the team in control commits a common foul, there will be no free-throws awarded. team-control also exists during a throw-in as it relates to the administering of a common foul.

Q2: Team A is in control of the ball when the ball becomes loose on the floor while A-1 commits a common foul on B-1. Team B is in the bonus. Since the ball was loose, the official awards B-1 a one and one free-throw. Is the official correct?

Y   N

Q1 Answer No. Since the ball has not been released by A-1 on this try for goal they are _not_ considered to be an airborne shooter.

Plan

PREGAME

Day / Date:

Location / Level / Tip Time:

Travel Time:

Leave By Time:

My Partner(s):

One thing I will try to do better in today's game is …

Assess

POSTGAME

What went well today?

Where did we get stuck today?

What will we do different next game?

YOUR PERFORMANCE ASSESSMENT					
Decision Accuracy	1	2	3	4	5
Floor Mechanics	1	2	3	4	5
Game Management	1	2	3	4	5
Rules Knowledge	1	2	3	4	5
Comportment	1	2	3	4	5

Pregame Conference Completed

Postgame Review Completed

$ _____

Fee Amount

Payment Received

Preparation

"I will prepare and someday my chance will come."

'Be careful of what you wish for, you just might get it,' is a cautionary warning that every official should heed. The desire to improve the quality of your assignments, and to advance to the next rung on your officiating ladder is natural and understandable. However, the secret to long term officiating success is to take the next step accompanied with the proper amount of game experience.

Undoubtedly, it's exciting to be considered one of the rising stars in your area; but more careers have been derailed by the 'cook it quick' microwave strategy, that it's worth pausing to ask if you are prepared to advance.

Warning for Delay

There are four types of delays that must be recorded in the scorebook and reported to the head coach when they occur. Only one warning is issued per team, per game for any of the four warnings.

Interfering with the ball following a goal is the most common. A team catching the ball after it goes through the net and placing it on the floor can be considered interference. The other common delay is reaching through the imaginary throw-in plane. Defenders can move right up to the sideline (or endline) but may not reach through the plane, even if no contact is made. Huddling by either team (and contacting the free-thrower) should be considered delay of game. The 4th type of delay is failure to have the court ready for play following any time-out. This can be for any situation that demands additional attention (i.e. spilled water) to extend a time-out. Any subsequent delays after the warning would result in an administrative technical foul.

Q3: In the 2nd quarter, Team A was issued a warning for delay of game when A3 reached through the plane. In the 3rd quarter team A was issued another warning for interfering with the ball after a goal. Since these were different warnings the official was correct?

Y   N

Q2 Answer : No. Remember, when a ball becomes loose it remains in control of the team that previously had control of it. This situation is typical when a ball gets away from the team and a foul occurs when trying to re-establish a dribble or pick up the loose ball. Fouls committed by the team in control are considered team-control fouls and would result in no free-throws awarded.

Plan

PREGAME

Day / Date:

Location / Level / Tip Time:

Travel Time:

Leave By Time:

My Partner(s):

One thing I will try to do better in today's game is ...

Assess

POSTGAME

What went well today?

Where did we get stuck today?

What will we do different next game?

YOUR PERFORMANCE ASSESSMENT					
Decision Accuracy	1	2	3	4	5
Floor Mechanics	1	2	3	4	5
Game Management	1	2	3	4	5
Rules Knowledge	1	2	3	4	5
Comportment	1	2	3	4	5

Pregame Conference Completed

Postgame Review Completed

$ _____
Fee Amount

Payment Received

Confidence

"Confidence is something you create within yourself by believing in who you are."

Carry yourself with a humble swagger and no one will ever confuse your confidence as arrogance. This officiating approach will convey to coaches, players and spectators that you are here to serve their needs; but that your kindness should not be confused as weakness.

The game has entrusted you with the authority to disqualify anyone from the contest, to eject anyone from the building and even forfeit the game. This amount of responsibility belongs only in the hands of an official who is confident enough in their own ability to *manage* disagreements, not escalate them.

Live Ball

The jump ball, the throw-in and the free-throw are the only methods of getting a dead ball to become live.

The concept of live ball / dead ball is important when it pertains to applying rules and penalties. Whenever an official blows the whistle the ball, almost always, is already dead because of a violation or foul and the sounding of the whistle, with proper signal, is primarily to alert the scorer to stop the clock. The ball becomes live when the ball leaves the official's hand during a jump ball. It also becomes live when it's at the disposal of the thrower for both a throw-in or free-throw. Disposal occurs when the ball is handed <u>or</u> is caught by the player after the official bounces the ball to them. Live ball and dead ball penalties vary, and officials should be cognizant of this status when applying them.

Q4: Team A just scored a goal. The ball is rolling near the endline for several seconds and near B1, when one of two scenarios occur: (a) A1 illegally contacts B1 or (b) A1 requests a time-out. Is the ball considered to be "dead" during these two situations?

Y   N

Q3 Answer : No. This second warning on the same team, even though it was for a different violation should result in a technical foul for that team. Subsequent violations (by the same team) after the first warning - even if they are different violations would result in a technical foul.

Plan

PREGAME

Day / Date:

Location / Level / Tip Time:

Travel Time:

Leave By Time:

My Partner(s):

One thing I will try to do better in today's game is ...

Assess

POSTGAME

What went well today?

Where did we get stuck today?

What will we do different next game?

YOUR PERFORMANCE ASSESSMENT					
Decision Accuracy	1	2	3	4	5
Floor Mechanics	1	2	3	4	5
Game Management	1	2	3	4	5
Rules Knowledge	1	2	3	4	5
Comportment	1	2	3	4	5

☐ Pregame Conference Completed

☐ Postgame Review Completed

$ _____
Fee Amount

☐ Payment Received

Resilient

"Life doesn't get easier or more forgiving, we get stronger and more resilient."

Stories of overnight successes are oftentimes actually works of fiction.

Upon closer examination, officials who appear to pop out of nowhere, actually stand on stacks of setbacks and heartbreaks, that could have, and perhaps should have, crushed their spirits.

But the resilient official bandages their bloody wounds and harnesses their determined spirit to get up and climb back in the fight. This means more meticulous practice and sharpening of skills to be ready for the big break that may be waiting just over the next hill.

Out of Bounds

Players are considered to be out of bounds when they touch the floor (or any other object) -- other than a player or person, that is on or outside a boundary line.

The official is directed to stop play when a ball touches (or is touched) by a player who is out of bounds. Any part of their body touching a boundary line, or beyond makes them out of play. A ball that touches the floor or other objects outside the boundary -- like the ceiling, backboard supports, overhead equipment, etc. is considered out of bounds.

If A1 who is dribbling the ball inbounds touches another player (or coach or bench personnel) when they are out of bounds does not cause the ball to be out of bounds. The ball remains live provided A1 did not touch a boundary line or other objects out of bounds.

Q5: While A2 is legally dribbling the ball inbounds, A2 inadvertently brushes up against the Team B coach while the coach was legally inside the coaching box. The official ruled this to be a legal play. Is the official correct?

Y   N

Q4 Answer : Yes and No, based on judgment. If the ball is judged to be at the thrower's disposal, the official should begin 5-second count and the ball is live. Meaning, no time-out would be granted and the illegal contact would be penalized. If no count was started and the ball remained dead, the illegal contact is ignored unless it's intentional or flagrant, the time-out would be granted.

Plan

PREGAME

Day / Date:

Location / Level / Tip Time:

Travel Time:

Leave By Time:

My Partner(s):

One thing I will try to do better in today's game is ...

Assess

POSTGAME

What went well today?

Where did we get stuck today?

What will we do different next game?

YOUR PERFORMANCE ASSESSMENT					
Decision Accuracy	1	2	3	4	5
Floor Mechanics	1	2	3	4	5
Game Management	1	2	3	4	5
Rules Knowledge	1	2	3	4	5
Comportment	1	2	3	4	5

Pregame Conference Completed

Postgame Review Completed

$ _____
Fee Amount

Payment Received

Failure

"You learn more from failure than from success."

If you are like most officials, the games that go smoothly seem to fade quickly from your memory bank or just all run together on one uneventful loop in your mind. But it is the painful details of the plays that you get wrong in a game, that may even have figured into the outcome of it, that stick with you.

Don't waste the pain of your mistakes. Autopsy them to learn everything about what brought you to the ruling, and then make a conscious effort to avoid that trap in future games.

Basket Interference

Can be caused by either the offensive or defensive players and results in the ball becoming dead immediately. If on the offense no points can be scored. If on the defense the goal is awarded.

Basket interference occurs when a player illegally touches the ball (or any part of the basket - including the net, flange, braces and ring) while the ball is <u>on or within</u> the basket. The ball becomes dead immediately. Touching the ball while any part of it is within the imaginary cylinder (above the basket ring) also is interference.

This includes touching the ball that is outside the cylinder but while reaching through the basket from below. If a player pulls down a collapsible basket ring so it contacts the ball before the ring returns to its original position, this is also considered interference. The penalty is based on who caused the interference.

Q6: While dunking the ball, A1's hand which started as legally in contact with the ball, entered the imaginary cylinder and subsequently touched the basket during the dunk. The official ruled basket interference and disallowed the goal. Was the official correct?

Y   N

Q5 Answer : Yes Touching a coach or player is legal provided A2 did not step on the boundary line or cause the ball to be out of bounds by other means.

Plan

PREGAME

Day / Date:

Location / Level / Tip Time:

Travel Time:

Leave By Time:

My Partner(s):

One thing I will try to do better in today's game is ...

Assess

POSTGAME

What went well today?

Where did we get stuck today?

What will we do different next game?

YOUR PERFORMANCE ASSESSMENT					
Decision Accuracy	1	2	3	4	5
Floor Mechanics	1	2	3	4	5
Game Management	1	2	3	4	5
Rules Knowledge	1	2	3	4	5
Comportment	1	2	3	4	5

☐ Pregame Conference Completed

☐ Postgame Review Completed

$ _____
Fee Amount

☐ Payment Received

Inspire

Enthusiasm

"Enthusiasm is the mother of effort, and without it nothing great was ever achieved."

You have chosen an avocation where almost every ruling you make is going to be questioned by half of the people playing or watching the game. This reality means you must be a self-starter and bring a high level of enthusiasm to every contest to counteract the negative energy that will flow to you unending waves.

Not false hustle or an insincere pollyanna demeanor; but rather a grounded positive energy that demonstrates you are genuinely happy to be working this game. This approach will set the right tone for most games, and will help blunt the negativity that anyone attempts to bring into a contest.

Learn

Closely Guarded

This situation occurs when a player in control of the ball (holding or dribbling) in their team's frontcourt is continuously guarded by an opponent who is within 6 feet of that player.

Designed to stimulate action and prevent the offensive from holding (or dribbling) the ball excessively in absence of a shot clock. The closely guarded situation should be observed by officials when appropriate.The 6 foot "closely guarded" distance between the players is measured from the forward foot of the defender to the forward foot of the player in control of the ball. When this occurs the official begins a closely guarded count that when 5 seconds is reached results in a violation. If a player is closely guarded when holding the ball then starts a dribble -- a new count is started. If they pick up the dribble and are closely guarded while holding the ball again, another fresh count is started. The count would be stopped when the offensive player (in control of the ball) gets their head and shoulders past the defensive player.

Challenge

Q7: A1 while dribbling is closely guarded by B1 for three seconds at which time A1 momentarily loses control of the ball. A1 subsequently resumed dribbling. The official started a new closely guarded count. Was the official correct?

Y   N

Q6 Answer : No. If a player has their hand legally in contact with the ball, it is not a violation if the contact with the ball continues after it enters the imaginary cylinder, or if the action causes the player to touch the basket. Dunking (or stuffing the basketball) is considered legal and not basket interference.

Plan

PREGAME

Day / Date:

Location / Level / Tip Time:

Travel Time:

Leave By Time:

My Partner(s):

One thing I will try to do better in today's game is ...

Assess

POSTGAME

What went well today?

Where did we get stuck today?

What will we do different next game?

☐ Pregame Conference Completed

☐ Postgame Review Completed

YOUR PERFORMANCE ASSESSMENT

Decision Accuracy	1	2	3	4	5
Floor Mechanics	1	2	3	4	5
Game Management	1	2	3	4	5
Rules Knowledge	1	2	3	4	5
Comportment	1	2	3	4	5

$ _____
Fee Amount

☐ Payment Received

Inspire

Compromise

The oak fought the wind and was broken, the willow bent when it must and survived.

In your journey for officiating self improvement, you are going to receive feedback and instruction from people whose opinion you respect, and some of it at times will seem to be contradictory.
Resist the urge to offer a, *"yeah, but I was told..."* reply to any well-intentioned critique.

With two seemingly different suggestions on positioning, mechanics, demeanor, etc. it is best to absorb it all and find a compromising balance that works for you. It is difficult to push back on any critique without appearing to be questioning the credibility of the instructor, so tread carefully in this area.

Learn

Wrong Basket

Mistakes are made by officials and can be fixed anytime. However specific errors where a rule is inadvertently set aside must be corrected within a specific "live ball - dead ball" timeframe.

If mistakenly the officiating crew allows a team to go (on offense) in the wrong direction, it can be fixed when discovered by stopping play and directing the teams to play in the proper direction based on their bench location. All points scored, fouls committed and time consumed shall count as if they team had gone in the proper direction.

Officials may correct an error if a rule is inadvertently set aside and results in a player attempting a free-throw at the wrong basket. This falls under "correctable errors" and must be recognized by an official no later than during the "first dead ball" timeframe after the clock has properly started.

Challenge

Q8: To start the 3rd quarter, Team A inbounds the ball and scores in the wrong basket. Team B subsequently goes in the wrong direction as well. The officials wait until the next stoppage of play to point the teams in the proper direction. Are the officials correct?

Y   N

Q7 Answer Yes. When A1's dribble was interrupted the player was no longer in control of the ball. Even if still closely guarded a new count would be started when A1 regained control and resumed the interrupted dribble.

Plan

PREGAME

Day / Date:

Location / Level / Tip Time:

Travel Time:

Leave By Time:

My Partner(s):

One thing I will try to do better in today's game is ...

Assess

POSTGAME

What went well today?

Where did we get stuck today?

What will we do different next game?

YOUR PERFORMANCE ASSESSMENT					
Decision Accuracy	1	2	3	4	5
Floor Mechanics	1	2	3	4	5
Game Management	1	2	3	4	5
Rules Knowledge	1	2	3	4	5
Comportment	1	2	3	4	5

☐ Pregame Conference Completed

☐ Postgame Review Completed

$ _____
Fee Amount

☐ Payment Received

Character

"The final forming of a person's character lies in their own hands."

A test of an official's true character is to take note of how they treat people associated with the game who are not in a position to help them. Don't be an official who spends your time and energy fawning over higher-rated referees, and ignoring, or even trying to stifle, those referees you view as potential competition to your standing within the organization. And be mindful of the character flaw in an official that allows a coach from a so-called elite program to run roughshod over them, while having a short fuse for a coach from a less successful school. Fortunes can change quickly, so officials should demonstrate their character by treating everyone with the same level of respect.

Teams and Captains

A team consists of five players to start the game, one of whom is the designated captain.

Games must begin with five players and are not permitted to start with less than five. Once the game is underway and a team has no substitutes to replace a disqualified or injured player, it must continue with fewer than five. When there is only one player participating for a team, the team must forfeit the game unless the referee believes that team has an opportunity to win the game.

The captain is a designated representative for their team that may address an official on matters of rule interpretation or to obtain essential information, if done in a courteous manner. This does not include questioning an official's ruling on judgment. Any player may address an official to request a time-out or request permission to leave the court.

Q9: Team A sends three bench players to the scorer's table waiting for the next dead ball opportunity to substitute. At this time Team B's captain asks the official if they can have a moment to match-up defenders with the substitutes. Can the official grant this request?

Y   N

Q8 Answer No. The officials should stop play when it's recognized the teams are going in the wrong direction. Waiting for a stoppage in play or a dead ball is not necessary. Use the point of interruption procedure to resume play with a throw-in by the team in control of the ball.

Plan

PREGAME

Day / Date: Location / Level / Tip Time:

Travel Time: Leave By Time:

My Partner(s):

One thing I will try to do better in today's game is ...

Assess

POSTGAME

What went well today?

Where did we get stuck today?

What will we do different next game?

YOUR PERFORMANCE ASSESSMENT					
Decision Accuracy	1	2	3	4	5
Floor Mechanics	1	2	3	4	5
Game Management	1	2	3	4	5
Rules Knowledge	1	2	3	4	5
Comportment	1	2	3	4	5

☐ Pregame Conference Completed   ☐ Postgame Review Completed

$ _____
Fee Amount

☐ Payment Received

Perseverance

"It doesn't matter how slowly you go as long as you do not stop."

Constructing a solid officiating career is like building a quality house -- the ones that are built with careful planning and sturdy material on a solid foundation will stand up to the strongest challenges and stand out as beacons of excellence. Fight the urge to get overly concerned about the pace of your officiating career advancement.

Keep building each phase of your referee development with care and forethought and you will be rewarded for your attention to detail. The slow but steady approach will eventually catch and pass the quick but stalled referee.

Guards, Casts and Braces

The officiating crew should not permit any team member to wear equipment or apparel that in their judgment is dangerous, confusing to other players or is not appropriate.

Guards, casts and braces are hard and unyielding and typically made of leather, plaster, plastic or metal. These items are not permitted to be worn on the elbow or below (i.e. wrist, hand, fingers). If worn above the elbow (forearm, shoulder, etc) the guard must be padded properly.

Knee and ankle braces (unmodified from the manufacturer) are permitted and do not require any additional padding. Hard protective face masks may be worn but must be molded to the face with no protrusions.All guards, casts and braces must be worn for medical reasons. No special documentation is required and typically the referee (or official) will ask the team member if the device if being used for medical reasons.

Q10: A7 reports into the game wearing a plastic forearm guard that is padded in such a way that in the judgment of the official it is not dangerous. The officials permits A7 to enter the game. Are the officials correct?

Y   N

Q9 Answer Yes, the official can grant this request. When three or more substitutes from the same team enter the game, a captain may request a defensive match-up. This should not delay the game and is done expeditiously.

Plan

PREGAME

Day / Date: _____   Location / Level / Tip Time: _____

Travel Time: _____   Leave By Time: _____

My Partner(s): _____

One thing I will try to do better in today's game is ...

Assess

POSTGAME

What went well today?

Where did we get stuck today?

What will we do different next game?

YOUR PERFORMANCE ASSESSMENT					
Decision Accuracy	1	2	3	4	5
Floor Mechanics	1	2	3	4	5
Game Management	1	2	3	4	5
Rules Knowledge	1	2	3	4	5
Comportment	1	2	3	4	5

☐ Pregame Conference Completed

☐ Postgame Review Completed

$ _____
Fee Amount

☐ Payment Received

Inspire

Growth

"It's only when you've stepped outside your comfort zone that you begin to change, grow and transform."

Staying the same will maintain your position of prominence is a lie that contented officials tell themselves in order to justify not putting in the work to improve. The cold hard truth is, you are either getting better or you're getting worse. There is no status quo.

There are too many referees working at their craft for your position to remain the same with each passing season. Age, energy level and physical conditioning are all factors eroding your officiating skills, and only with a conscious commitment to getting better can you earn the type of schedule you expect.

Learn

Extra Period

Typically referred to as "overtime," an extra period is actually an extension of playing time in the fourth quarter that is needed to break a tie score.

In scholastic contests the length of each extra period is 4 minutes -- <u>or</u> half the time of a regulation quarter for non-varsity contests. If the score is tied additional periods are added. There is also no change of baskets (team direction) for any extra period. Always allow a one minute intermission before starting any period.

The game must be played until one team is ahead at the expiration of the extra period. Once the ball becomes live in any extra period it MUST be played (all the way through) even if a scoring correction is made from a previous quarter - including the 4th quarter.

Challenge

Q11: During the first dead ball in the extra period of play, the officials notice the clock shows 4:20 remaining. The scorer recalls starting with 5 minutes. To rectify this, the crew subtracts the extra minute and the game resumes with 3:20 on the clock. Is this correct?

Y   N

Q10 Answer No. Hard or unyielding guards/ braces are not permitted to be worn on (or below) the elbow. Regardless of the padding presented by A7 and the personal judgment of the official regarding safety, by rule this is not permitted and the player must either remove the brace or not be permitted to enter the game.

Plan

PREGAME

Day / Date: Location / Level / Tip Time:

Travel Time: Leave By Time:

My Partner(s):

One thing I will try to do better in today's game is ...

Assess

POSTGAME

What went well today?

Where did we get stuck today?

What will we do different next game?

YOUR PERFORMANCE ASSESSMENT

Decision Accuracy	1	2	3	4	5
Floor Mechanics	1	2	3	4	5
Game Management	1	2	3	4	5
Rules Knowledge	1	2	3	4	5
Comportment	1	2	3	4	5

☐ Pregame Conference Completed   ☐ Postgame Review Completed

$ _____ Fee Amount

☐ Payment Received

Discipline

"Discipline is the refining fire in which talent becomes a reality."

The adage, *"you get out of it what you put into it"* certainly holds true for building an officiating career. Identifying the goal and detailing the action steps for success is the easy part.
Having the discipline to follow the plan that will have you mentally and physically prepared to be recognized as an elite official, is another matter entirely.

When it is all said and done, if there more said than actually done, it will simply mean that the winds of your words were stronger than fire in your spirit. Discipline will fan the fire that will forge your greatness.

Resumption-of-Play

When a team does not make a player (thrower) available after a time-out or intermission a specific procedure called the "resumption-of- play" shall be used by the officials.

The resumption-of-play procedure is as follows:
1. The administering official sounds the whistle to signal play is about to resume.
2. If the throwing Team (A) is not ready, place the ball on the floor and begin the 5 second count.
3. If a violation occurs award the ball to Team B. If team B fails to provide a player to throw the ball in the same procedure is repeated for Team B. Place the ball on the floor and begin the 5 second count.
4. If both teams violate and still do not provide a player for the throw-in --- any further delay (by either team) is a technical foul. Officials should be judicious if the teams are trying to comply after a time-out or intermission.

Q12: Team A does not break the huddle after the 2nd horn for a 60-second time-out. The official places the ball on the floor and begins the 5 second count. B-1 reaches through the boundary and picks up the ball? Official permits this action as the ball is live. Is the official correct?

Y   N

Q11 Answer No. In an extra period where a timing mistake occurs, you should follow these guidelines.
If the mistake is discovered before the clock reaches the proper period length (4 minutes), then resume play with the clock set at 4 minutes. If discovered after, then no correction is allowed. The clock should have been set to 4 minutes to resume play.

Plan

PREGAME

Day / Date:

Location / Level / Tip Time:

Travel Time:

Leave By Time:

My Partner(s):

One thing I will try to do better in today's game is …

Assess

POSTGAME

What went well today?

Where did we get stuck today?

What will we do different next game?

YOUR PERFORMANCE ASSESSMENT					
Decision Accuracy	1	2	3	4	5
Floor Mechanics	1	2	3	4	5
Game Management	1	2	3	4	5
Rules Knowledge	1	2	3	4	5
Comportment	1	2	3	4	5

☐ Pregame Conference Completed

☐ Postgame Review Completed

$ _____
Fee Amount

☐ Payment Received

Inner Strength

"Strength does not come from physical capacity. It comes from an indomitable will."

Whether we learn more from failure than we do from success has been debated for years. Frankly, any consensus of opinion is irrelevant when bitter disappointment lands at your officiating doorstep. The only thing that matters is if you have the inner strength to struggle to get back on your feet after absorbing the knockdown of rejection as you try to move up within your organization. And then move beyond it. Officiating is not for the weak of spirit or spine. Before you can have your judgment questioned by coaches, players and spectators, you must first convince the assignor that you have the intestinal fortitude to succeed.

Baskets

The baskets are comprised of several components. This includes the 18 inch (inside diameter) metal ring, it's flanges and braces, along with the whited-corded net that hangs below the ring.

In any violation that refers to "touching the basket," officials are reminded that all of these components make up the "basket." The ring, flange and braces must be orange in color.

The net should be constructed in such a way the ball is "checked" momentarily as a ball passes through from above - but does not stop the ball from completely passing through. When a net is "whipped" or tangled on the ring (or braces) the official should direct a player to toss the ball into the net as to allow the net in returning to a normal position. This situation should not require a stoppage in live-ball play and may be done during the next dead ball.

Q13: During Team A's try for goal, the ball passes through the ring and becomes stuck in a whipped net which the officials did not notice. A-2 jumps and touches the ball while it remains in the net and the official rules basket interference. Is this correct?

Y   N

Q12 Answer No, the official is not correct. This is a delay-of-game warning for Team B for reaching across the plane. Team A had not possessed the ball (for the throw-in) therefore a technical foul would not be assessed.

Plan

PREGAME

Day / Date:	Location / Level / Tip Time:
Travel Time:	Leave By Time:

My Partner(s):

One thing I will try to do better in today's game is ...

Assess

POSTGAME

What went well today?

Where did we get stuck today?

What will we do different next game?

YOUR PERFORMANCE ASSESSMENT

Decision Accuracy	1	2	3	4	5
Floor Mechanics	1	2	3	4	5
Game Management	1	2	3	4	5
Rules Knowledge	1	2	3	4	5
Comportment	1	2	3	4	5

☐ Pregame Conference Completed

☐ Postgame Review Completed

$ _____
Fee Amount

☐ Payment Received

Focus

"The successful warrior is the average man with laser-like focus."

You have to feed your focus and starve your distractions. Now your faith, your family and your employer are not distractions, so they should be given priority over your officiating. But everything else in your life should be fair game to be put on a severe time limit diet.

And when officiating is on the front burner, be sure you are not distracted by the petty politics and gossip that often plagues organizations. Your focus needs to be on improving your on court skills and enhancing your off court officiating relationships.

Dunking

Driving, forcing, pushing or attempting to force the ball through the basket with the hands is considered a dunk.

A player, while dunking, should be considered in the act of shooting the ball.

If fouled during the act of dunking the goal may be awarded (provided the ball passes through or remains in the basket) with the appropriate free-throws to follow.

Grasping and hanging on the the ring during a dunk is permitted provided the officials rule this act is to prevent injury. Touching the basket on the follow through while the ball is passing through is not considered a violation.

Q14: During an attempted dunk by airborne shooter A-1, the ball becomes loose. Player A1 subsequently grasps the ring to prevent injury after losing control of the ball. The official rules a technical foul, as A1 was not actually dunking the ball. Is the official correct?

Y   N

Q13 Answer No. A ball that passes through and remains in the basket is considered to be a scored goal. In this case with A-2 touching the dead ball would be ignored, as they are not intentionally trying to delay the game. It would be wise for the official to sound the whistle and clarify the play to the official scorer if needed.

Plan

PREGAME

Day / Date: Location / Level / Tip Time:

Travel Time: Leave By Time:

My Partner(s):

One thing I will try to do better in today's game is ...

Assess

POSTGAME

What went well today?

Where did we get stuck today?

What will we do different next game?

YOUR PERFORMANCE ASSESSMENT					
Decision Accuracy	1	2	3	4	5
Floor Mechanics	1	2	3	4	5
Game Management	1	2	3	4	5
Rules Knowledge	1	2	3	4	5
Comportment	1	2	3	4	5

☐ Pregame Conference Completed

☐ Postgame Review Completed

$ _____
Fee Amount

☐ Payment Received

Inspire

Poise
The key to winning is poise under stress.

A famous boxer once said that, *"everybody has a plan on how to beat me until I punch them in the face."* Well, as an official you need to be prepared for that moment in game when tensions erupt and you suddenly feel the weight of the players, coaches and spectators bearing down on you.

An official with some degree of game experience can often sense the escalation and perhaps defuse the situation. But if you are passed the point of prevention, you will need to get ABOVE the fray and not be IN it. This will require a practiced mindset of poise under pressure to calmly monitor and manage the situation.

Learn

Player-Control
A player is considered to be "in control" when they are holding or dribbling a live ball.

"Holding" a ball occurs when it's grasped by one or both hands, placed under the arm by the player. The ball must be live to be considered in the player's control. A player is not in control while slapping the ball during a jump, when a pass rebounds from the hands, when they fumble the ball or when a pass (or rebound) is batted away from them. Additionally when a players' dribble is interrupted they are no longer in control (but there is still team-control).

Neither player-control (or team-control) exists during a dead ball or when the ball is in flight for a try (or tap) for goal.

Challenge

Q15: A-1 is holding the ball in the backcourt when A-1 reaches out and pushes B1 to gain space. Team B is in the bonus. The official rules this as a player-control foul and awards the ball to team B. Is the official correct?

Y   N

Q14 Answer No. Even though player A1 lost control of ball during this play, they are permitted to grasp the Ring to prevent injury, provided this is not considered an unsportsmanlike act. Players should be permitted to grasp the ring to provide a safer return to the floor after being airborne. The official should have allowed this play to proceed without penalty.

Plan

PREGAME

Day / Date: Location / Level / Tip Time:

Travel Time: Leave By Time:

My Partner(s):

One thing I will try to do better in today's game is ...

Assess

POSTGAME

What went well today?

Where did we get stuck today?

What will we do different next game?

YOUR PERFORMANCE ASSESSMENT

Decision Accuracy	1	2	3	4	5
Floor Mechanics	1	2	3	4	5
Game Management	1	2	3	4	5
Rules Knowledge	1	2	3	4	5
Comportment	1	2	3	4	5

☐ Pregame Conference Completed

☐ Postgame Review Completed

$ _____
Fee Amount

☐ Payment Received

Inspire

Courage

"Mistakes are always forgivable, if you have the courage to admit them. "

If you officiate long enough, there will come an inevitable moment in a game where a decision you make in the closing minutes will have a direct impact on its outcome. Your decision to call or pass on a foul or violation happened, as they all do, in flash and you immediately regret the choice made.

This great game is played, coached and officiated by imperfect people. You can't change your decision; you just have to make peace with it. So find the balance between being totally dismissive of the error without learning from it, and being crushed to the point that it affects you in future contests.

Learn

Jump Ball

The jump ball is one of three methods of getting a dead ball to become live. The throw-in and free-throw are the other two. It's used to start play at the beginning of the game and each overtime period.

The referee (or designated official) tosses the ball at the center restraining circle, between any two opponents to initiate the jump ball procedure. The ball becomes live when the jump ball begins as it leaves the official's hand for the toss. The jump ends when the ball is contacted by a non-jumper, the floor, the basket or the backboard.

The umpire (tableside) is directed to start (and chop) the clock when the ball is legally touched by the jumpers. A held ball is commonly referred to as a jump ball but is actually when two players have their hands so firmly on the ball, neither player can gain control without undue roughness.

Challenge

Q16: During a jump ball, jumper A-1 touches the ball simultaneously with both hands followed by the right hand then followed by the left hand. The official rules this a violation since the ball was touched three times. Is the official correct?

Y   N

Q15 Answer Yes. player-control fouls apply when a player in control fouls an opponent. No free-throws are awarded and the offended team is given the ball for an ensuing designated spot throw-in at the spot closest to the foul.

Plan

PREGAME

Day / Date: Location / Level / Tip Time:

Travel Time: Leave By Time:

My Partner(s):

One thing I will try to do better in today's game is ...

Assess

POSTGAME

What went well today?

Where did we get stuck today?

What will we do different next game?

<table>
<tr><th colspan="6">YOUR PERFORMANCE ASSESSMENT</th></tr>
<tr><td>Decision Accuracy</td><td>1</td><td>2</td><td>3</td><td>4</td><td>5</td></tr>
<tr><td>Floor Mechanics</td><td>1</td><td>2</td><td>3</td><td>4</td><td>5</td></tr>
<tr><td>Game Management</td><td>1</td><td>2</td><td>3</td><td>4</td><td>5</td></tr>
<tr><td>Rules Knowledge</td><td>1</td><td>2</td><td>3</td><td>4</td><td>5</td></tr>
<tr><td>Comportment</td><td>1</td><td>2</td><td>3</td><td>4</td><td>5</td></tr>
</table>

☐ Pregame Conference Completed

☐ Postgame Review Completed

$ _____
Fee Amount

☐ Payment Received

Gratitude

"Gratitude is not only the greatest of all virtues, it is the parent of all the others."

When the urge to waste precious time and energy worrying about other officials who appear to be advancing faster than you, take a moment to reflect on what you have, and not on what you don't. The fact of the matter is that every game you were healthy enough in mind and body to step on the court to officiate a game, no matter what the level of play, was a gift.

Rather than grousing about the peers who seem to be passing you by, or the new officials who are gaining on you, let a spirit of gratitude smother your greed. You likely can easily call to mind several officials who had their careers abruptly ended due to illness, injury or even death.

Possession Arrow

A visible mechanism shall be located at the scorer's / timer's table that indicates team possession for the purpose of the alternating-possession procedure.

The team gaining possession from a jump ball determines how the possession arrow will be set. The team not obtaining possession has the arrow pointed toward their basket direction and will receive the ball to start the next regulation period or in the case of a held ball. Once the throw-in has ended the possession arrow is reversed to point in the opposite direction.

An alternating-possession (AP) throw-in is different than a typical throw-in. If there is a foul during the AP throw-in, the subsequent throw-in is not part of the original AP throw-in AND the arrow is not changed. The only way a team loses the arrow during an AP throw-in is if the throwing team commits a violation.

Q17: The AP arrow is pointing toward Team A's basket. By mistake the official awards Team B the ball to start the 2nd quarter. B1 releases the throw-in and it is touched by B2 when the official recognizes this mistake. The official blows the whistle. Is the official correct?

Y   N

Q16 Answer Yes. Touching the ball with two hands simultaneously counts as touching the ball once. Next, touching of the ball by the left hand followed by the right hand resulted in "three touches." Jumpers are permitted to touch the ball twice but not three times. This results in a violation.

Plan

PREGAME

Day / Date:

Location / Level / Tip Time:

Travel Time:

Leave By Time:

My Partner(s):

One thing I will try to do better in today's game is ...

Assess

POSTGAME

What went well today?

Where did we get stuck today?

What will we do different next game?

YOUR PERFORMANCE ASSESSMENT					
Decision Accuracy	1	2	3	4	5
Floor Mechanics	1	2	3	4	5
Game Management	1	2	3	4	5
Rules Knowledge	1	2	3	4	5
Comportment	1	2	3	4	5

☐ Pregame Conference Completed

☐ Postgame Review Completed

$ _____
Fee Amount

☐ Payment Received

Inspire

Respect

"One of the most sincere forms of respect is actually listening to what another has to say."

Officials should be conscious of conveying a fair but firm demeanor when dealing with players and coaches. You will want to monitor that your kindness and respectful tone is not viewed as weakness and results in you being talked to in a disrespectful and dismissive manner.

The game always belongs to the players, and the coaches oversee the players for the enjoyment of the spectators -- but you and your partners have been hired to manage the game and get it to its conclusion.. A confident, courteous temperament with firm and consistent rulings will set the proper tone.

Learn

Tap

The tap is the contacting of the ball with any part of a player's hand(s) in an attempt to direct the ball into their basket. The tap is similar to a try for goal as it relates to when a foul occurs.

A tap starts when a player's hand(s) touches the ball and ends (similar to a try) when the ball clearly leaves the player's hand(s). Studies confirm that a player cannot catch the ball and subsequently release it on a try (for goal) when three-tenths (0.3) of a second or less show on the clock. Therefore officials should be cognizant of the clock situation when there is less than one second left and there is a free-throw or throw-in. In this situation where there is three-tenths of a second or less on the clock, the player cannot score a goal after gaining control of the ball. In this situation only a "tap" would be permitted to score a goal. This rule does not apply when the scoreboard or clock does not display tenths of a second.

Challenge

Q18: A1 taps the ball and the ball enters the basket after time expires. The official rules this is a legal goal and two points are scored. The opposing coach questions the referee as the tap must enter the basket before time expires. Was the official correct?

Y   N

Q17 Answer No. Once the throw-in ends, it's too late to fix this official's mistake. Since the ball was touched by B2 inbounds the throw-in was completed. The official should allow play to continue and the AP arrow will continue to point toward A's basket. Team A will receive the next alternating-possession throw-in.

Plan

PREGAME

Day / Date:

Location / Level / Tip Time:

Travel Time:

Leave By Time:

My Partner(s):

One thing I will try to do better in today's game is ...

Assess

POSTGAME

What went well today?

Where did we get stuck today?

What will we do different next game?

YOUR PERFORMANCE ASSESSMENT					
Decision Accuracy	1	2	3	4	5
Floor Mechanics	1	2	3	4	5
Game Management	1	2	3	4	5
Rules Knowledge	1	2	3	4	5
Comportment	1	2	3	4	5

☐ Pregame Conference Completed

☐ Postgame Review Completed

$ _____
Fee Amount

☐ Payment Received

Inspire

Wisdom

"Knowing yourself is the beginning of all wisdom."

Are your officiating goals realistic? While it's true your reach should always exceed your grasp; you want to make sure that what you're striving for is attainable.

The higher the level you hope to reach in officiating, the more scrutiny your age, gender and body type will receive. You want to find a healthy balance between maximizing your ability and enjoying the challenge of striving for a lofty goal, but not setting yourself up for disappointment.

Learn

Simultaneous Touch

If a ball goes out of bounds and was last touched simultaneously by two opponents the officials shall resume play by the team entitled to the alternating-possession arrow.

To provide fairness the two players who caused the ball to go out of bounds are held responsible - even though no control was established. For this situation to occur both players must be inbounds when simultaneously touching the ball.

In addition, if the officials are in doubt on which player caused the ball to go out of bounds or if the officials disagree then the alternating-possession procedure would we used to determine which team is awarded the ball for a throw-in. If the A-P arrow has not been established yet then a jump ball between the two players that simultaneously touched the ball will be used to resume play.

Challenge

Q19: To start the first overtime period following the jump ball between A1 and B1, the ball is touched simultaneously by A2 and B2 before rolling out of bounds. The referee re-administers the jump ball between A1 and B1 to start the overtime properly. It the official correct?

Y   N

Q18 Answer Yes. Despite the opposing coach's pleas, the goal should be counted. A tap is similar for a try (for goal) provided the ball leaves the "tapper's" hand before the expiration of time. The official is correct here.

Plan

PREGAME

Day / Date:

Location / Level / Tip Time:

Travel Time:

Leave By Time:

My Partner(s):

One thing I will try to do better in today's game is ...

Assess

POSTGAME

What went well today?

Where did we get stuck today?

What will we do different next game?

☐ Pregame Conference Completed

☐ Postgame Review Completed

YOUR PERFORMANCE ASSESSMENT					
Decision Accuracy	1	2	3	4	5
Floor Mechanics	1	2	3	4	5
Game Management	1	2	3	4	5
Rules Knowledge	1	2	3	4	5
Comportment	1	2	3	4	5

$ _____
Fee Amount

☐ Payment Received

Ambition

"Intelligence without ambition is like a bird without wings."

Ambivalence and a blase attitude may be chic in some circles, but it won't take you far in officiating. Consider developing a mindset that demonstrates you believe it is cool to hustle, to be prepared, in shape and on time for everything you do.

This approach is made more attainable and more enjoyable by making it a point to associate with like-minded officials. Your fellow officials who are not willing to make the same commitment to rule competency, physical conditioning and time management will view you as a threat to disrupting their lazy routine.

Noisemakers

In the spirit of fairness and sportsmanship, artificial noisemakers are prohibited at all times.

While fans and supporters are permitted to scream and yell within "sportsmanlike" boundaries, the use of artificial devices are not permitted in the stands at any time. Officials should bring this to the attention of the on-site administrator for the activity to cease and remove the noisemaker.

The playing of music (live or recorded) and sound effects are permitted only during pregame, time-outs, intermissions, and post-game.

If these situations, persist a technical foul may be administered, but clearly as a last resort.

Q20: A1 is dribbling on a breakaway for an easy lay-up when a fan blows a whistle from the stands which causes A1 to stop. B1 steals the ball before the referee can stop play. The officials use the point of interruption, awarding Team A the ball to resume play. Is this correct?

Y   N

Q19 Answer No. Since the alternating-possession procedure (and arrow) have not been established to start the overtime period the simultaneous touching of A-2 and B-2 will result in a jump ball between the two players that caused the ball to go out of bounds. A-2 and B-2 shall jump from the center restraining circle to start the overtime.

Plan

PREGAME

Day / Date:

Location / Level / Tip Time:

Travel Time:

Leave By Time:

My Partner(s):

One thing I will try to do better in today's game is ...

Assess

POSTGAME

What went well today?

Where did we get stuck today?

What will we do different next game?

YOUR PERFORMANCE ASSESSMENT					
Decision Accuracy	1	2	3	4	5
Floor Mechanics	1	2	3	4	5
Game Management	1	2	3	4	5
Rules Knowledge	1	2	3	4	5
Comportment	1	2	3	4	5

☐ Pregame Conference Completed

☐ Postgame Review Completed

$ _____
Fee Amount

☐ Payment Received

Humility

"True humility is not thinking less of yourself; it is thinking of yourself less."

Do not confuse having a humble servant's spirit with having low self-esteem.

It is the officials in every organization who can blend the right amount of modesty and confidence into their demeanor when interacting with their partners, coaches and players, that make it to the top in this avocation. The secret to GETTING the quantity and quality of games you seek, lies in how much you are GIVING of yourself.

This means means being a servant to the game and understanding that your interests are best met when the work you provide allows the game to be managed fairly and shine brightly.

Legal Guarding Position

A guard must have both feet touching the playing court (inbounds) along with the guard's front torso facing the opponent to establish the initial "legal" guarding position.

Once the initial legal position has been legally obtained, the defender may have one or both feet on the court or airborne - provided they have inbound status. The defender is not required to continue facing the opponent and may additionally move laterally or obliquely (on an angle) to maintain the initial legal position - provided they do not move forward which causes contact.

Defenders are also permitted to raise their hands or jump within their own vertical plane or even turn (and duck) to absorb the shock of contact. Once a legal guarding position is established, the player with the ball must get their head and shoulders past the torso of the defensive player. If contact occurs on the torso of the defender, the dribbler is responsible for the contact.

Q21: A1 is dribbling near the sideline when defender B1 obtains a legal guarding position. B1 moves backward and in doing so has one foot touching the sideline when A1 contacts B1 in the torso. The official rules a blocking foul on B1. Is the official correct?

Y   N

Q20 Answer Yes. The officials should utilize the POI when the artificial noisemaker caused the disruption in play. While A1 should ignore sounds from the stands, a whistle obviously caused the player to stop and provided an unfair advantage to Team B. If not able to be located, an announcement can be made that future violations may result in a technical foul.

Plan

PREGAME

Day / Date:

Location / Level / Tip Time:

Travel Time:

Leave By Time:

My Partner(s):

One thing I will try to do better in today's game is ...

Assess

POSTGAME

What went well today?

Where did we get stuck today?

What will we do different next game?

YOUR PERFORMANCE ASSESSMENT					
Decision Accuracy	1	2	3	4	5
Floor Mechanics	1	2	3	4	5
Game Management	1	2	3	4	5
Rules Knowledge	1	2	3	4	5
Comportment	1	2	3	4	5

☐ Pregame Conference Completed

☐ Postgame Review Completed

$ _____
Fee Amount

☐ Payment Received

Inspire

Commitment

"Commitment is an act, not a word."

People are too busy watching what you are doing to be listening to what you are saying. Your deeds will hold your words hostage and make you accountable to follow through on the promises you make to others and to your own goals for personal growth. Your firm resolve is the bridge your goals must travel to carry them over the obstacles and distractions to achieve success.

There is both strength and freedom in the word, "NO," so use it confidently to lift your priorities above the clutter that will bog you down and hinder your ability to honor the important commitments in your life.

Learn

Goaltending

Is a violation when a defender touches a ball during a field-goal or free-throw while on its downward flight, is above the level of the basket ring, and has a possibility of going in the basket.

For goaltending to occur there are several criteria that must be assessed very quickly by the officials.
1) The play must be a legitimate try for goal (or free-throw).
2) When touched by the defender, the ball must be above the level of the ring, on its downward flight and must be outside the imaginary cylinder.
3) The try must also have a legitimate chance of going through the basket if not touched.

This violation results in the scoring of the try (2pts or 3pts) or free-throw (1pt). In addition a technical foul is assessed for goaltending during a free-throw and can occur on upward or downward flight.

Challenge

Q22: A1's 3-point try is in flight when the horn sounds for the expiration of the 4th quarter. Clearly after the horn sounds B1 goaltends on A1's try and the official allows the play to continue as the ball became dead after the horn sounded. Is the official correct?

Y   N

Q21 Answer Yes. This is a blocking foul as B1 must keep both feet inbounds to establish, or in this case, maintain a legal guarding position. Defenders are permitted to move backward and obliquely to maintain this position.

PREGAME

Day / Date:

Location / Level / Tip Time:

Travel Time:

Leave By Time:

My Partner(s):

One thing I will try to do better in today's game is ...

POSTGAME

What went well today?

Where did we get stuck today?

What will we do different next game?

☐ Pregame Conference Completed

☐ Postgame Review Completed

YOUR PERFORMANCE ASSESSMENT

	1	2	3	4	5
Decision Accuracy	1	2	3	4	5
Floor Mechanics	1	2	3	4	5
Game Management	1	2	3	4	5
Rules Knowledge	1	2	3	4	5
Comportment	1	2	3	4	5

$ _____
Fee Amount

☐ Payment Received

Purpose

"The meaning of life is to find your gift. The purpose of life is to give it away."

The earlier you learn in your career that officiating is more than just racking up bigger game fees, the more rewarding your journey as a referee will be. Give strong consideration to sharing your officiating talents with charitable organizations in their fundraising efforts. Make yourself available to share your experience and knowledge, with a mentoring spirit, with your fellow officials, particularly those just getting started.

More good things will come to you when your arms are open, than when they are closed with tight fists.

Bench Personnel / Team Members

Bench personnel are individuals that are part of the team or affiliated with a team. If in uniform and eligible to become a player, these bench personnel are considered team members.

Bench personnel include coaches, managers, statisticians, athletic trainers, and substitutes on the bench -- that are affiliated with the team. If in uniform and eligible to enter the game they are considered team members. The key distinction applies to the administration of a technical foul.

Any technical foul given to bench personnel also results in an indirect technical foul against the head coach. A player becomes bench personnel after their substitute becomes a player or after the head coach is notified following their disqualification. During an intermission all team members are considered bench personnel for the purpose of penalizing unsporting behavior.

Q23: Following A2's fifth personal foul, the official notifies Team A's head coach of A-2's disqualification. During the replacement interval, A-2 shares unsporting comments with an opponent. The official ignores these actions as they are already disqualified. Is this correct?

Y   N

Q22 Answer : No. The expiration of time and horn sounding does not cause A1's try to become dead. The goaltending violation by B1 should be penalized by awarding A1 a 3pt goal. Officials should sound their whistle and report the violation to the scorer's table properly.

PREGAME

Day / Date: Location / Level / Tip Time:

Travel Time: Leave By Time:

My Partner(s):

One thing I will try to do better in today's game is …

POSTGAME

What went well today?

Where did we get stuck today?

What will we do different next game?

☐ Pregame Conference Completed   ☐ Postgame Review Completed

YOUR PERFORMANCE ASSESSMENT

	1	2	3	4	5
Decision Accuracy	1	2	3	4	5
Floor Mechanics	1	2	3	4	5
Game Management	1	2	3	4	5
Rules Knowledge	1	2	3	4	5
Comportment	1	2	3	4	5

$ _____
Fee Amount

☐ Payment Received

Goal

"A goal properly set is halfway reached."

If the officiating goal you have for yourself doesn't challenge you, there won't be enough incentive to maximize your abilities. Make sure you have set a goal worthy of your best efforts, then concentrate on the action steps needed to reach it. This strategy will keep you from focusing on the obstacles you will undoubtedly encounter.

If your plan to achieve your officiating goal is not bringing you the results on the timetable you have set, then change your plan, but not the goal. You have put the time in to set the proper goal -- stay with it!

Guarding a Moving Opponent

Whether the opponent has the ball or not will determines if time and distance should be considered when contact is made.

When guarding a moving opponent WITHOUT the ball, both time and distance are factors required when establishing an initial legal guarding position. The defender must give the opponent both time and distance to avoid contact. This distance need not be more than two normal strides.

If an opponent has the ball or is not moving, then NO time or distance is required when establishing a legal guarding position. If an opponent is airborne, the defender must obtain a legal guarding position before the opponent left the floor.

Q24: Defender B1 attempts to take a guarding position on A1 who is airborne. A1 makes contact directly in B1's torso while returning to the floor. The official rules a player-control foul against A1 since B1 had a legal guarding position. Is the official correct?

Y   N

Q23 Answer No. Once A2 is disqualified and Team A's coach is notified they become, "bench personnel." Any actions by A2 should be penalized and carry additional penalty of an indirect technical foul for Team A's coach. This foul would be recorded and count toward the bonus situation. If utilized, the head coach would lose the coaching box privilege.

Plan

PREGAME

Day / Date:

Location / Level / Tip Time:

Travel Time:

Leave By Time:

My Partner(s):

One thing I will try to do better in today's game is ...

Assess

POSTGAME

What went well today?

Where did we get stuck today?

What will we do different next game?

YOUR PERFORMANCE ASSESSMENT					
Decision Accuracy	1	2	3	4	5
Floor Mechanics	1	2	3	4	5
Game Management	1	2	3	4	5
Rules Knowledge	1	2	3	4	5
Comportment	1	2	3	4	5

Pregame Conference Completed

Postgame Review Completed

$ _____
Fee Amount

Payment Received

Inspire

Trust

"Once you earn trust it's priceless; but once you lose it you are useless."

Coming to the realization that your officiating partners are the only friends you have in a game, will be a painful lesson if you have to learn it the hard way. Don't ever do or say anything to undermine your fellow officials' credibility within your organization or with a coach, player or spectator.

Being guilty of such conduct in our avocation is a serious offense and it is a broken bond that may be forgiven, but likely won't ever be forgotten. Don't do anything that will cause you to lose the trust of the only true friends you have in the game.

Learn

Backcourt Violation

Once the offensive team has advanced the ball into the frontcourt, they are not permitted to touch the ball in the backcourt if their team was the last to touch it in their frontcourt.

To obtain frontcourt status a player dribbling must have both feet and the ball entirely in the front court. Remember, the division line is considered to be part of the backcourt!

A player cannot be the first to touch a ball after it has been in team-control in the frontcourt, if their teammate last touched the ball (or the ball touched them) in the frontcourt before it went into the backcourt. A player is not permitted to cause the ball to go from backcourt to frontcourt and return again to the backcourt. A defensive player, or any player on a jump-ball or throw-in, may legally jump from frontcourt, then secure control of the ball with both feet off the floor and land in the backcourt - without penalty.

Challenge

Q25: A1 catches the throw-in pass with one foot on the floor in A's frontcourt and the other foot not touching the floor. The non-pivot foot then touches down in A's backcourt. The official rules a backcourt violation. Is the official correct?

Y   N

Q24 Answer No. For B1 to obtain a legal guarding position, they must do this prior to A1 leaving the floor to become airborne. The official should rule a blocking foul on B1.

Plan

PREGAME

Day / Date:

Location / Level / Tip Time:

Travel Time:

Leave By Time:

My Partner(s):

One thing I will try to do better in today's game is ...

Assess

POSTGAME

What went well today?

Where did we get stuck today?

What will we do different next game?

YOUR PERFORMANCE ASSESSMENT					
Decision Accuracy	1	2	3	4	5
Floor Mechanics	1	2	3	4	5
Game Management	1	2	3	4	5
Rules Knowledge	1	2	3	4	5
Comportment	1	2	3	4	5

☐ Pregame Conference Completed

☐ Postgame Review Completed

$ _____
Fee Amount

☐ Payment Received

Tenacity

"Most things worth doing in the world had been declared impossible before they were done."

Any negative assessment of your officiating skills only becomes cemented in reality when you accept it as fact. Until that moment, the outcome of how far you can advance and how good you can become, should be marked as, 'status to be determined.'

Many sporting event wagers have been lost betting on the more talent team or athlete over the more tenacious one. Don't let the key to your officiating happiness be kept in the pocket of anyone else but you!

Throw-In After Goal

After a successful goal, the opponents are permitted to make a throw-in from any point along the endline from the end of the court where the goal was made.

After a score, it is legal for the throw-in team to run along the endline or pass the ball to a teammate out of bounds on the endline, within the 5-second limitation.

If the scoring team commits a violation or common foul before the throw-in ends - provided the bonus rule is not in effect - the throwing team retains this right, provided the throw-in spot would have been on the same endline. Any player of the team may legally make the throw-in, run along the endline with the ball, dribble the ball completely out of bounds or even pass the ball to a teammate(s) outside the endline boundary.

Q26: While Team A's three-point field-goal attempt is in flight, A3 fouls B1. Team B is not in the bonus. The three-point field goal is successful. The official scores the goal and Team B is permitted to move along the endline on the ensuing throw-in. Correct?

Y   N

Q25 Answer Yes. This is a backcourt violation. Both team-control and player-control are established in A's frontcourt when the throw-in pass is caught by A1. When the pivot foot touches down in the backcourt this causes a violation. If A1 would have jumped from the frontcourt, caught the ball in the air and landed in the backcourt --- that would have been legal.

Plan

PREGAME

Day / Date:

Location / Level / Tip Time:

Travel Time:

Leave By Time:

My Partner(s):

One thing I will try to do better in today's game is …

Assess

POSTGAME

What went well today?

Where did we get stuck today?

What will we do different next game?

☐ Pregame Conference Completed

☐ Postgame Review Completed

YOUR PERFORMANCE ASSESSMENT					
Decision Accuracy	1	2	3	4	5
Floor Mechanics	1	2	3	4	5
Game Management	1	2	3	4	5
Rules Knowledge	1	2	3	4	5
Comportment	1	2	3	4	5

$ _____
Fee Amount

☐ Payment Received

Patience

"Trees that are slow to grow bear the best fruit."

Over the years the pace of advancement in officiating has quickened significantly, so it becomes easier to get discouraged if it appears your career movement has stalled. However, it is critical to maintain control of what you can about the situation, and that is to be patiently persistent with a positive and professional attitude.

Sulking and/or complaining rarely ever helps an official move forward. Now that is not to imply that you should not respectfully push back with direct questions on the reason for your current status. Just be prepared for direct answers!

Alternating-Possession (AP) Situations

There are eight alternating-possession situations that invoke the use of the AP arrow.

1. A Held Ball.
2. Double Fouls - either Personal or Technical and only if there is <u>no</u> team-control.
3. The official (or crew) is unsure (or cannot agree) who caused the ball to go out of bounds.
4. Simultaneous Free-Throw Violations -- by opponents.
5. The ball becomes lodged on a basket support.
6. Opponents commit Simultaneous Personal or Technical Fouls and only if there is <u>no</u> team-control.
7. The ball becomes dead and neither team is in control -- and no goal is scored -- and no infraction or end of period is involved.
8. Opponents commit simultaneous Goaltending or Basket-Interference violations.

Q27: The AP arrow is pointing toward B's basket. While A-1 is dribbling the ball, A2 and B2 foul each other at approximately the same time. The official penalizes both players and awards Team B the ball for an ensuing AP arrow throw-in. Is the official correct?

Y   N

Q26 Answer Yes. Since Team B is not in the bonus they are permitted to move along the endline on the ensuing throw-in.

Plan

PREGAME

Day / Date: Location / Level / Tip Time:

Travel Time: Leave By Time:

My Partner(s):

One thing I will try to do better in today's game is ...

Assess

POSTGAME

What went well today?

Where did we get stuck today?

What will we do different next game?

☐ Pregame Conference Completed   ☐ Postgame Review Completed

YOUR PERFORMANCE ASSESSMENT					
Decision Accuracy	1	2	3	4	5
Floor Mechanics	1	2	3	4	5
Game Management	1	2	3	4	5
Rules Knowledge	1	2	3	4	5
Comportment	1	2	3	4	5

$ _____
Fee Amount

☐ Payment Received

Clarity

"It's the lack of clarity that creates chaos and confusion. These emotions are poison to any goal."

Do you know what you want from your officiating career?

If a mentor or a person of influence responds favorably to your request for help, what will your reply be to the question, *"how can I help you?"* Do not make the person extending the helping hand do all of the heavy lifting. Be ready with a well thought out answer that is as reasonable as it is specific. People who possess the clout to improve your life are more inclined to help an official with a clearly defined goal with a clearly stated request.

Clock Starts

One of the on-court officials has the responsibility of signaling to the scorer's table when the clock should properly be started. However, it is still the timer's responsibility to start the clock properly.

The clock should be "chopped" in by an official as follows:
- On the <u>jump ball</u> ... when the tossed ball is legally touched by one (or both) of the jumpers.
- On the <u>free-throw</u> ... if not successful and the ball is to remain live, when the ball touches (or is legally touched) by a player on the court.
- On the <u>throw-in</u> ... when the ball touches or is legally touched by a player on the court after it is released by the thrower.

Officials should report on-court starting their jurisdiction no later than 15 minutes prior to game time.

Q28: With two seconds left on the clock, Team A is awarded two free-throws. After the second free-throw the ball caroms off the ring and rolls out of bounds without any player touching it. The clock now shows 0.6 seconds remaining. The official awards Team B the ball. Correct?

Y   N

Q27 Answer No. Since Team A was in control of the ball when the double foul occurred then Team A would be permitted to retain possession under the point-of-interruption. If neither team had control, then the officials would be correct in using the AP arrow procedure to determine which team get possession for the ensuing throw-in.

PREGAME

Day / Date: Location / Level / Tip Time:

Travel Time: Leave By Time:

My Partner(s):

One thing I will try to do better in today's game is …

POSTGAME

What went well today?

Where did we get stuck today?

What will we do different next game?

☐ Pregame Conference Completed   ☐ Postgame Review Completed

YOUR PERFORMANCE ASSESSMENT

	1	2	3	4	5
Decision Accuracy	1	2	3	4	5
Floor Mechanics	1	2	3	4	5
Game Management	1	2	3	4	5
Rules Knowledge	1	2	3	4	5
Comportment	1	2	3	4	5

$ _____
Fee Amount

☐ Payment Received

Dedication

"Talent is cheap; dedication is expensive. It will cost you your life."

Absent illness or injury and work or family restrictions, your officiating success is ultimately going to come down to the amount of preparation and hard work you put into your craft.

The more single-minded effort you expend to reach your goal, the less nourishment that will be available to feed the excuses most associated with failure (i.e organizational politics; age, race, gender, etc.) And remember, it is the dedicated work done in the quiet solitary moments studying the rulebook and conditioning your body that prepares you to be chosen for the big games in the large crowded gyms in front of screaming fans.

Free-Thrower

When free-throw(s) are awarded because of a personal foul, they must be attempted by the offended player, unless that player must withdraw because of injury or disqualification.

If a player cannot attempt the free-throw(s) -- their substitute must attempt the throw(s). In the event there are no eligible substitutes left, any teammate may attempt the throw(s). That team's head coach or captain may choose who attempts these.

Free-throws awarded resulting from a Technical Foul may be attempted by ANY player of the offended team -- including eligible substitute, designated starters or any player in the game at this time. The coach or captain can designate this free-thrower.

Q29: Team B is awarded two free-throws as the result of a technical foul. Team B coach chooses B-3 to attempt the free-throws. After missing the first free-throw the coach asks the official to allow B-5 to attempt the second. The official grants this request. Is this correct?

Y   N

Q28 Answer No. The clock was not started properly. The ball must be touched by a player on the floor for the clock to start. Since the officials had definite knowledge of time remaining prior to the free-throw, they should instruct the timer to place the time back on the clock and award Team B the ball with 2.0 seconds left.

Plan

PREGAME

Day / Date:

Location / Level / Tip Time:

Travel Time:

Leave By Time:

My Partner(s):

One thing I will try to do better in today's game is ...

Assess

POSTGAME

What went well today?

Where did we get stuck today?

What will we do different next game?

YOUR PERFORMANCE ASSESSMENT					
Decision Accuracy	1	2	3	4	5
Floor Mechanics	1	2	3	4	5
Game Management	1	2	3	4	5
Rules Knowledge	1	2	3	4	5
Comportment	1	2	3	4	5

☐ Pregame Conference Completed

☐ Postgame Review Completed

$ _____
Fee Amount

☐ Payment Received

Adaptable

"The measure of intelligence is the ability to change."

Old ways will not open new doors; so your mind and spirit must be as flexible as your body in order to stay current and valued as an official. Be ready and willing to implement updated mechanics and revised interpretations of rules into your game with a positive attitude.

That means being prepared to leave your stubborn veteran peers behind to run with the ever-changing herd. There is ample evidence in the evolution of our world that it is not the strongest or smartest species that survives. It is the ones who are most adaptable to change.

Scorer's Duties

The official scorer is required to wear a black-and-white vertically striped garment and recommended to be situated at the scorer's table, near the division line.

The scorer is responsible for many facets of the "administrative" components for the game. This includes keeping a record of the names and numbers of players who are to start the game and all the substitutes who enter the game. The scorer should also notify the nearer official when there is an infraction of the rules pertaining to submission of the roster, substitutions or the number of players.

Keeping the running score (tally), recording fouls and time-outs are also duties of the scorer. They are also responsible for keeping track and movement of the alternating-possession arrow. If a player is disqualified they should notify the nearest official.

Q30: Team A's coach goes to the table while play is going on and the ball is live to request a stoppage of play for a potential correctable error. The scorer sounds the horn while Team A is on a breakaway and the official stops play to confer with the scorer. Is the official correct?

Y   N

Q29 Answer Yes. The official would be correct in allowing a different team member to attempt each of the free-throws, provided they are eligible as a substitute or already in the game.

PREGAME

Plan

Day / Date: Location / Level / Tip Time:

Travel Time: Leave By Time:

My Partner(s):

One thing I will try to do better in today's game is …

POSTGAME

Assess

What went well today?

Where did we get stuck today?

What will we do different next game?

Pregame
Conference
Completed

Postgame
Review
Completed

YOUR PERFORMANCE ASSESSMENT					
Decision Accuracy	1	2	3	4	5
Floor Mechanics	1	2	3	4	5
Game Management	1	2	3	4	5
Rules Knowledge	1	2	3	4	5
Comportment	1	2	3	4	5

$ _____

Fee Amount

Payment Received

Service

"The best way to find yourself is to lose yourself in the service of others."

It is easy to fall into the trap of ranking/rating your assignments and, perhaps subconsciously, portioning out your energy and focus based on the level of the game and the importance of the contest. Whether you are just starting your officiating career, or a veteran referee in need of changing some bad habits, begin today to challenge yourself to treat each assignment with a consistent positive attitude. And if you find this an easier said than done task, consider for a moment that a person who could influence your officiating career just might be in attendance at that next low level, seemingly meaningless, game you are working. Referee that game, and every one after it as if this is your big audition. Because it just might be!

Swinging Elbows Violation

It is not legal to swing one's arms and elbows excessively, even if there is no contact made with an opponent.

'Excessive' is defined as when the arms and elbows are swung about while using the shoulders as pivots --- and the speed is in excess of the rest of the body, as it rotates on the hips (or pivot foot). This is a violation.

This aggressive and dangerous activity should be penalized whenever it is observed before it causes an injury from contact. It is legal for a player to hold the ball under the chin (or against the body) with the arms/elbows extended. Normal pivoting or movement of the ball incidental to faking with it, or releasing the ball on a pass should not be considered excessive. Causing contact while excessively swinging elbows results in a foul to be ruled.

Q31: A1 taps the ball toward their basket. While the ball is in flight, B2 excessively swings his elbows but does not make contact with anyone. After the tap is successful the official sounds the whistle, scores the goal and awards Team A the ball. Is this correct?

Y   N

Q30 Answer No. If the scorer signals while the ball is live, the official should ignore the signal if an apparent scoring play is in progress. If not, the official may stop play to determine the reason for the scorer's signal. If the official stops play inadvertently, they may resume play with POI procedure or the alternating-possession arrow if no team is in possession of the ball.

Plan

PREGAME

Day / Date:

Location / Level / Tip Time:

Travel Time:

Leave By Time:

My Partner(s):

One thing I will try to do better in today's game is ...

Assess

POSTGAME

What went well today?

Where did we get stuck today?

What will we do different next game?

Pregame Conference Completed

Postgame Review Completed

YOUR PERFORMANCE ASSESSMENT

Decision Accuracy	1	2	3	4	5
Floor Mechanics	1	2	3	4	5
Game Management	1	2	3	4	5
Rules Knowledge	1	2	3	4	5
Comportment	1	2	3	4	5

$ _____

Fee Amount

Payment Received

Virtue

"The man who does not value himself, cannot value anyone or anything."

The barrage of criticism that an official often has to endure means that you need to bring a solid foundation of self-respect into this avocation. If you don't, the game will ultimately change your demeanor for the worse.

You will be able to withstand the outcry of dissent about your rulings, if you go into each game mentally and physically prepared and give your best effort. The heat of athletic competition can produce a great deal of ugly behavior and without a strong sense of self-worth you will absorb the loud critical comments as personal attacks.

Clock Stops

When running, the clock is primarily stopped when an official signals a foul, a held ball, or a violation.

Additionally, the clock should be stopped when an official halts play because of an injury or a player is bleeding. The official may signal to stop the clock when a player or head coach orally (or visually) requests a time-out.

The clock is also stopped when the scorer / timer needs to confer with the officiating crew. The clock always remains stopped during time-outs, intermission and any unusual delays in getting a dead ball live or for any other emergency situations. Officials may use judgement when stopping play for an injury and allow the play to finish first if not dangerous or if a player is not in any immediate danger.

Q32: B1's dribble is interrupted when the ball deflects off B-1's foot. The coach quickly verbally requests a time-out and the official grants this this based on the fact Team B maintained team-control during the interrupted dribble. Is the official correct?

Y   N

Q31 Answer Yes the official is correct. The ball does not become dead until the try (or tap in this situation) ends or the airborne shooter returns to the floor, when there is a violation by the opponent. The goal should be scored and Team A is awarded the ball at the nearest spot to the violation for an ensuing throw-in.

Plan

PREGAME

Day / Date:

Location / Level / Tip Time:

Travel Time:

Leave By Time:

My Partner(s):

One thing I will try to do better in today's game is ...

Assess

POSTGAME

What went well today?

Where did we get stuck today?

What will we do different next game?

YOUR PERFORMANCE ASSESSMENT					
Decision Accuracy	1	2	3	4	5
Floor Mechanics	1	2	3	4	5
Game Management	1	2	3	4	5
Rules Knowledge	1	2	3	4	5
Comportment	1	2	3	4	5

☐ Pregame Conference Completed

☐ Postgame Review Completed

$ _____
Fee Amount

☐ Payment Received

Balance

"Balance is not something you find. It's something you create."

Success can be intoxicating.
And the more you achieve, the easier it can be to rationalize focusing on the source of it at the expense of other areas. With officiating, you have to always be vigilant to not put your family relationships, or your full-time job at risk to chase the allure of making it to the next level.

Enjoy the game for the quality relationships it can create, and for the outlet it can be. Do not let your family or your job become casualties of your misaligned officiating priorities.

Free-Throw Timing

The try for goal must be made within 10 seconds after the ball has been placed at the disposal of the free-thrower at the free-throw line.

In an effort to speed up the game, the respective committees governing the rules believe 10 seconds is sufficient time to gather one's composure after being fouled and attempt a free-throw. This applies to each of multiple free-throws awarded.

During this try the ball must enter the basket or touch the ring or backboard before the free-throw ends. The trail official (or center official in a crew of 3) is directed to maintain a visible count using a small wrist-flick to enforce this rule.

Q33: A1 has the ball at her disposal for a free-throw and the official has counted up through 8 seconds before A1 requests a time-out. The official grants this request. Is the official correct?

Y   N

Q32 Answer No. While there is team-control during an interrupted dribble, there is no player-control which is required to grant a time-out request. In this case the official should "hold" their whistle until a player of Team B regains control.

PREGAME

Plan

Day / Date:

Location / Level / Tip Time:

Travel Time:

Leave By Time:

My Partner(s):

One thing I will try to do better in today's game is ...

POSTGAME

Assess

What went well today?

Where did we get stuck today?

What will we do different next game?

YOUR PERFORMANCE ASSESSMENT					
Decision Accuracy	1	2	3	4	5
Floor Mechanics	1	2	3	4	5
Game Management	1	2	3	4	5
Rules Knowledge	1	2	3	4	5
Comportment	1	2	3	4	5

☐ Pregame Conference Completed

☐ Postgame Review Completed

$ _____
Fee Amount

☐ Payment Received

Loyalty

"In the end, we will remember not the words of our enemies, but the silence of our friends."

In this age of social media, the misfortunes of a fellow official -- or your own -- can spread through the basketball community like wildfire. Don't be an official that enjoys being part of a gossip session that shares a cruel laugh at the expense of another referee's misery.

Take a higher road, and be the official who helps to extinguish a disparaging war story with your silence or purposely changing the topic. And be the referee who always offers an unpatronizing word of encouragement to an official in need.

Dribble

The dribble is ball movement caused by a player (who in control) throws, bats or pushes the ball to the floor, once or several times.

To be legal, the dribble must be started (out of the dribblers hand) prior to the pivot foot being lifted from the floor. The ball may be batted into the air provided it is permitted to strike the floor before the ball is touched again with the hands. It is not a part of a dribble when the ball touches the player's own backboard.

The dribble ends when the player catches or causes the ball to rest in one or both hands; simultaneously touches the ball with both hands; or the ball touches an opponent which causes the dribbler to lose control. The dribble also ends when the ball becomes dead. It is not possible (by rule) for a player to travel during a dribble.

Q34: A1's dribble strikes a hard spot on the floor and bounces higher than A1's head. A1 continues to dribble while keeping the hand on top of the ball and pushing it back down toward the floor. The official rules this as an illegal dribble. Is this correct?

Y   N

Q33 Answer Yes. Provided the count did not reach 10-seconds, any player or coach from the free-thrower's team may request, and be granted, a time-out.

PREGAME

Day / Date:

Location / Level / Tip Time:

Travel Time:

Leave By Time:

My Partner(s):

One thing I will try to do better in today's game is ...

POSTGAME

What went well today?

Where did we get stuck today?

What will we do different next game?

YOUR PERFORMANCE ASSESSMENT

Decision Accuracy	1	2	3	4	5
Floor Mechanics	1	2	3	4	5
Game Management	1	2	3	4	5
Rules Knowledge	1	2	3	4	5
Comportment	1	2	3	4	5

☐ Pregame Conference Completed

☐ Postgame Review Completed

$ _____
Fee Amount

☐ Payment Received

Influence

"Success isn't just about what you accomplish in your life. It's what you inspire others to do."

'To whom much is given, much will be required,' is a reminder and a challenge that is as old as the Bible. If you happen to be one of the top officials in your organization, you have a moral imperative to set a consistently high standard of excellence for matters of punctuality, attitude, appearance, etc. on and off the court.

Being a person of influence in your association, means you will help set the tone and demeanor for what is acceptable in terms of conduct and attitude. If you are one of the "Big Dogs" in your organization, its reputation and good name is in your hands.

Personal Foul

A foul is an infraction of the rules which is charged and penalized. Personal fouls involve illegal contact with an opponent while the ball is live which hinders them from normal movements.

Personal fouls can also include contact by (or on) an airborne shooter when the ball is dead. Contact after the ball has become dead should be considered "incidental" unless it is intentional or flagrant -- or on an airborne shooter. Players are disqualified from participation upon receiving their 5th personal foul or any flagrant personal foul.

No free-throws for common (personal) fouls are awarded prior to the bonus rule being in effect. The offended team is permitted to make a throw-in from the designated spot out-of-bounds nearest the foul location.

Q35: Prior to the bonus rule being in effect, B2 commits a common foul by grasping A1 during a field-goal try, but after A1 has completed the act of shooting. The goal is successful. The official scores the goal and awards Team A the ball out of bounds. Is this correct?

Y   N

Q34 Answer No, provided the dribbler did not allow the ball come to rest in the one hand. The high dribble while it may look strange is completely legal if A1 did not violate any of the dribbling provisions. In this case they did not.

Plan

PREGAME

Day / Date:

Location / Level / Tip Time:

Travel Time:

Leave By Time:

My Partner(s):

One thing I will try to do better in today's game is ...

Assess

POSTGAME

What went well today?

Where did we get stuck today?

What will we do different next game?

YOUR PERFORMANCE ASSESSMENT					
Decision Accuracy	1	2	3	4	5
Floor Mechanics	1	2	3	4	5
Game Management	1	2	3	4	5
Rules Knowledge	1	2	3	4	5
Comportment	1	2	3	4	5

☐ Pregame Conference Completed

☐ Postgame Review Completed

$ _____
Fee Amount

☐ Payment Received

Accountable

"It is not only what we do, but what we do not do, for which we are accountable."

As an official you have a primary coverage area (PCA) on the floor that you are responsible for monitoring. But there is an overlapping PCA that you are responsible for watching, no matter where you are positioned on the court, and that is your partner's back.

You want to give your partner the respect and freedom to handle their own business when a ruling they make triggers a dispute with a player or coach. But do not allow anyone to take advantage of your partner's good nature, or if you believe they are struggling with the heat of the moment. Be an official who is accountable to yourself and to your partners.

Blocking

Illegal personal contact which impedes the progress of an opponent, with or without the ball, is considered blocking.

To maintain the balance between defense and offense -- opponents are not permitted to illegally "block" each other while moving on the floor. This allows for the freedom of movement and to not affect the rhythm, speed, balance and quickness of any player.

Dribblers have more burden placed upon them and are not permitted to charge (or contact) an opponent that established a legal guarding position. If a dribbler gets both head and shoulders past the torso of a defender and contact occurs, a blocking foul should be ruled. The defender is permitted to hold their hands (and arms) in front of their face or body for protection, and to absorb force from an imminent charge by an opponent.

Q36: B1 is standing underneath the backboard before A1 jumps for a lay-up. The momentum (airborne) causes A1 to charge into B1. The official rules a blocking foul since the defender was not permitted to guard the opponent from underneath the basket. Is this correct?

Y   N

Q35 Answer Yes, the official is correct. The common foul committed by B2 does not cause the ball to become dead. The official ruled correctly by scoring the goal and awarding the ball to Team A at the designated spot nearest to where the foul occurred.

Plan

PREGAME

Day / Date: Location / Level / Tip Time:

Travel Time: Leave By Time:

My Partner(s):

One thing I will try to do better in today's game is ...

Assess

POSTGAME

What went well today?

Where did we get stuck today?

What will we do different next game?

YOUR PERFORMANCE ASSESSMENT					
Decision Accuracy	1	2	3	4	5
Floor Mechanics	1	2	3	4	5
Game Management	1	2	3	4	5
Rules Knowledge	1	2	3	4	5
Comportment	1	2	3	4	5

☐ Pregame Conference Completed

☐ Postgame Review Completed

$ _____
Fee Amount

☐ Payment Received

Guidance

"Live your life and forget your age."

Everyone gets on the officiating train at different stations, but do not let your age deter you from getting on and taking the ride in this rewarding avocation. If you are older, the ride may not be as long and you may have missed the opportunity for some higher quality stops. But you will be proud of all you see and do.

If you are a younger official, the early part of the journey may seem uninteresting, but it is going to be a long ride, so sit up, take plenty of detailed notes and lock in the great mental pictures. Young or old - this ride will be what you make it!

Intentional Fouls

An intentional fouls is a personal (or technical foul) that may or may not be premeditated.

Fouls that neutralize an opponent's obvious advantageous position away from the ball - when that opponent is clearly not involved in the play should be ruled intentional. Contact that is not a legitimate attempt to play the ball or specifically designed to stop the clock (or keep it from starting) is also intentional. Excessive contact with an opponent while the ball is live or until an airborne shooter returns to the floor should be ruled intentional. A defender reaching through the boundary line plane and fouling an opponent during a throw-in is considered an intentional foul. If the thrower reaches through and is fouled it is still considered an intentional foul. The penalty is two free-throws plus the ball for a throw-in awarded to the offended player and team.

Q37: A1 is driving to the basket when B1 intentionally fouls A1. The try is successful. The official scores the goal and assesses B1 with an intentional foul. A1 is awarded two free-throws and the ball at the nearest spot to the foul for a throw-in. Is the official correct?

Y   N

Q36 Answer No, this should be ruled a charge on the airborne shooter A1. While some rule codes vary on this, for scholastic (NFHS) games, the defender is permitted to establish a legal guarding position anywhere on the floor (inbounds). Being underneath the basket has no bearing on this requirement. See other codes for differences.

Plan

PREGAME

Day / Date: Location / Level / Tip Time:

Travel Time: Leave By Time:

My Partner(s):

One thing I will try to do better in today's game is ...

Assess

POSTGAME

What went well today?

Where did we get stuck today?

What will we do different next game?

YOUR PERFORMANCE ASSESSMENT

Decision Accuracy	1	2	3	4	5
Floor Mechanics	1	2	3	4	5
Game Management	1	2	3	4	5
Rules Knowledge	1	2	3	4	5
Comportment	1	2	3	4	5

Pregame
Conference
Completed

Postgame
Review
Completed

$ _____
Fee Amount

Payment Received

Inspire

Good Health

"If you think the pursuit of good health is expensive and time consuming, try illness."

In the blink of an eye, your officiating career can be taken from you because of injury or illness, so you would be wise to appreciate the quality and quantity of games you are receiving. There is no guarantee you will officiate another game -- ever -- no matter what your assignor has put on your scheduling plate.

You can make a vital contribution to determining the length of your career by maintaining your ideal body weight and staying consistent with your cardio conditioning. And by avoiding the self-inflicted wounds of careless behavior.

Learn

Marked Lane Spaces

There are three marked lane spaces on each lane boundary line. They extend 36 inches from the outer edge of the lane lines toward the sidelines. A maximum of 6 players may occupy these spaces.

The first two lane spaces (nearest the endline) must be occupied by the opponent of the free-thrower or a violation has occurred. Players may not have either foot beyond the vertical plane of any lane space edges. The second marked lane spaces may be first occupied by the teammate of the free-thrower. The third marked lane spaces nearest the free-thrower may be first occupied by the opponents of that free-thrower. Vacancies in the second and third spaces may be occupied by either team. These players are permitted to enter the lane area after the free-thrower releases the ball for the try.Other players not in marked lane spaces must be behind the free-throw line extended and the three-point arc. These players must not break this plane until the ball strikes the ring or backboard.

Challenge

Q38: During A1's free-throw attempt, B1 and B2 are occupying the first marked lane spaces. Team A's players are refusing to occupy the 2nd marked spaces. The official tells the captain of Team A they must have players in these spaces. Is the official correct?

Y   N

Q37 Answer Yes, the official is correct. The intentional foul carries its own penalty. Regardless of the outcome, for A1's try for goal -- A1 is awarded two free-throws. Team A is also awarded a designated spot throw-in nearest to where the foul was ruled.

Plan

PREGAME

Day / Date:

Location / Level / Tip Time:

Travel Time:

Leave By Time:

My Partner(s):

One thing I will try to do better in today's game is ...

Assess

POSTGAME

What went well today?

Where did we get stuck today?

What will we do different next game?

YOUR PERFORMANCE ASSESSMENT					
Decision Accuracy	1	2	3	4	5
Floor Mechanics	1	2	3	4	5
Game Management	1	2	3	4	5
Rules Knowledge	1	2	3	4	5
Comportment	1	2	3	4	5

Pregame Conference Completed

Postgame Review Completed

$ _____
Fee Amount

Payment Received

Inspire

Inspiration

"Everything you can imagine is real."

No one is going to drag you towards your dream.

You may be fortunate enough to have someone in your life who believes in your officiating skills and who will steadily prod you to do all that you can to be the best you can be.

But at the end of the day, it is going to be up to you to find the inspiration ignition switch and flip it each and every day. If you can conceive it, you can achieve it.

The question only you can answer is, will you put in the work to make your dream a reality?

Learn

Throw-In Plane

This is an imaginary line that extends from the boundary line (nearest edge toward the floor inbounds) vertically toward the ceiling.

The throw-in plane provides separation from the team inbounding the ball and the defenders. This natural buffer, if broken by the defending team (by reaching through), results in a delay-of-game warning for the first offense. If any further warnings (of any kind) are issued, the team is assessed a technical foul. However once the ball is released, the defender may reach (or step) through the plane. If the thrower reaches through with the ball, the defender may legally steal it. Teammates of the thrower are also NOT permitted to reach through the plane and receive the throw-in --- unless it's after a successful goal and that team is permitted to move along the endline. In this case, they are permitted to pass the ball to a teammate(s) out of bounds provided the throw-in is completed within 5 seconds.

Challenge

Q39: Team B while defending a throw-in reaches through the imaginary throw-in plane but does not make contact with the thrower. The official ignores this action as it is not flagrant or intentional. Is the official correct?

Y   N

Q38 Answer No. Only the first two marked lane spaces must be occupied. Additionally, they must be occupied by the opponents of the free-thrower. Officials should direct the teams to occupy these spaces before administering the free-throw as to avoid a violation.

Plan

PREGAME

Day / Date:

Location / Level / Tip Time:

Travel Time:

Leave By Time:

My Partner(s):

One thing I will try to do better in today's game is ...

Assess

POSTGAME

What went well today?

Where did we get stuck today?

What will we do different next game?

Pregame
Conference
Completed

Postgame
Review
Completed

YOUR PERFORMANCE ASSESSMENT

Decision Accuracy	1	2	3	4	5
Floor Mechanics	1	2	3	4	5
Game Management	1	2	3	4	5
Rules Knowledge	1	2	3	4	5
Comportment	1	2	3	4	5

$ _____

Fee Amount

Payment Received

Opportunity

"The Chinese use two brush strokes to write the word 'crisis.' One brush stroke stands for danger; the other opportunity. In a crisis, beware aware of the danger -- but recognize the opportunity. "

There are many veteran officials who have achieved a measure of success in the game who will tell you their careers were given an unexpected boost from an unforeseen set of circumstances. Having a spare referee bag packed and stashed in your car will undoubtedly increase your odds of being able to answer the call out of the stands, or out the blue by a frantic assignor looking for an able replacement for an injured or late official.

And if the assignment just happens to be a little above your comfort level; so much the better to fire that booster rocket of opportunity!

Kicking Violations

Kicking is intentionally striking the ball with any part of the leg or foot.

The key word here is, "intentional." The action of the ball striking the leg or foot does not necessarily mean a kicking violation has occurred. The player must intentionally kick at, and make contact with the ball, for this to be ruled.

If the ball happens to come in contact with the foot or leg of player who DID NOT make an attempt to kick the ball, this is NOT a violation, and play should be allowed to continue. Additionally, a kicking violation can be ruled against the team (or player) in control, if ruled an intentional act. The offended team shall receive the ball for a designated spot throw-in nearest to the spot of the violation.

Q40: While defending A1's pass to A2, the ball caroms off B1's thigh and goes out of bounds. The official awards Team A the ball for a throw-in for B1 causing the ball to go out of play and not a kicking violation. Is the official correct?

Y   N

Q39 Answer No. When a defender reaches through the throw-in plane the official should first issue a team warning for delay of game. Subsequent warnings (for that team of any kind) will result in a technical foul being awarded to the offending team.

Plan

PREGAME

Day / Date:

Location / Level / Tip Time:

Travel Time:

Leave By Time:

My Partner(s):

One thing I will try to do better in today's game is ...

Assess

POSTGAME

What went well today?

Where did we get stuck today?

What will we do different next game?

YOUR PERFORMANCE ASSESSMENT					
Decision Accuracy	1	2	3	4	5
Floor Mechanics	1	2	3	4	5
Game Management	1	2	3	4	5
Rules Knowledge	1	2	3	4	5
Comportment	1	2	3	4	5

☐ Pregame Conference Completed

☐ Postgame Review Completed

$ _____
Fee Amount

☐ Payment Received

Inspire

Education

"Education is an ornament in prosperity and a refuge in adversity."

You may at some point find yourself in a group setting with other officials and hear a referee, usually a veteran official, say, *"I'm not a rules person."*

This foolish boast arrogantly proclaims to all within earshot that a legitimate claim can be made for a career advancement strategy that relies on people skills and a 'feel for the game.' Under no uncertain terms should you give this approach a second thought. It is a ticking time bomb and it will eventually go off and the crew will pay the price for one official's laziness when it comes to learning the rules.

Learn

Inadvertent Whistle

When an official sounds their whistle inadvertently there are ways to get underway quickly by knowing where the point of interruption was.

Whenever you or a crew member accidentally blows a whistle, the ball becomes dead immediately, with the exception of a few situations. The ball remains live if a try (or tap) is in flight toward the goal. Also the ball remains live if a foul is committed by any opponent on a player who has started that tap (or try) before a foul occurred. In this situation, it is provided that time did not expire before the ball was in flight.

In all situations, the ball is put back in play at the point of interruption. If no team-control exists, the crew should utilize the alternating-possession procedure to resume play. Otherwise, just pick-up where you inadvertently stopped play.

Challenge

Q41: A1's 3 point try is in flight from near the division line. The official inadvertently sounds their whistle during the try thinking a foul occurred. After discussing as a crew they award Team B the ball, as they rebounded the missed try. Are the officials correct?

Y   N

Q40 Answer Yes, the official is correct. The action by B1 was not deemed intentional, so therefore no kicking violation was ruled. The ball did go out of bounds and was last touched by B1 which resulted in the same effect.

Plan

PREGAME

Day / Date: Location / Level / Tip Time:

Travel Time: Leave By Time:

My Partner(s):

One thing I will try to do better in today's game is ...

Assess

POSTGAME

What went well today?

Where did we get stuck today?

What will we do different next game?

YOUR PERFORMANCE ASSESSMENT					
Decision Accuracy	1	2	3	4	5
Floor Mechanics	1	2	3	4	5
Game Management	1	2	3	4	5
Rules Knowledge	1	2	3	4	5
Comportment	1	2	3	4	5

☐ Pregame Conference Completed

☐ Postgame Review Completed

$ _____
Fee Amount

☐ Payment Received

Truth

"All truths are easy to understand once they are discovered; the key is to discover them."

Often times there is a difference between what is the truth is, and the truth as you know it.
One is fact, and the other lives as an opinion of one or more people.
With this in mind, you should be guarded in sharing a negative opinion about a fellow official or coach.
Your critical assessment of someone may also be held by others, but your opinion offered up behind their back does nothing to elevate the conversation.
And perhaps more importantly, it will likely have people wondering what you think of them when they are not around.

Point of Interruption (POI)

The POI is a way to determine how the officials should resume play when stopped under special circumstances.

These situations include an official's inadvertent whistle, an interrupted game, a correctable error, a double foul (either personal or technical) and finally a simultaneous foul. In all these scenarios, the crew should pay attention to which team was in control at the time of the interruption. When the POI is invoked, play should be resumed with a throw-in by the team that was in control at the nearest spot to where the ball was located at the moment of the interruption. If the interruption occurs during a free-throw or throw-in, the play will be resumed by that action. Officials are reminded the ball remains live during an inadvertent whistle while a try (or tap) for goal is in flight. The POI is then determined to be when the ball becomes dead following the violation or foul.

Q42: While A2 is dribbling near the division line, the lead official rules a double foul on players A1 and B1 while jockeying for position inside the lane area. The officials report the fouls and resume play with Team A's throw-in near the division line. Is this correct?

Y   N

Q41 Answer   No. The inadvertent whistle did not cause the ball to become dead immediately as a try for goal was in flight. Since there is no team-control during the try -- the point of interruption must be determined by the alternating-possession procedure. Awarding Team B the ball because they rebounded the try would not be correct. The crew should utilize the AP arrow to determine which team is entitled to the ensuing throw-in.

PREGAME

Day / Date: Location / Level / Tip Time:

Travel Time: Leave By Time:

My Partner(s):

One thing I will try to do better in today's game is ...

POSTGAME

What went well today?

Where did we get stuck today?

What will we do different next game?

YOUR PERFORMANCE ASSESSMENT

Decision Accuracy	1	2	3	4	5
Floor Mechanics	1	2	3	4	5
Game Management	1	2	3	4	5
Rules Knowledge	1	2	3	4	5
Comportment	1	2	3	4	5

☐ Pregame Conference Completed

☐ Postgame Review Completed

$ _____
Fee Amount

☐ Payment Received

Willingness

"Where the willingness is great, the difficulties cannot be great."

Rare is the official who has not had to face some obstacles to continue their referee avocation. Now whether the source of the challenge is related to demands coming from your job or from your home life, the solution is no doubt a personal one. But if your desire to continue to officiate holds a high place on your priority list, often there are compromises that can be implemented to serve both masters.

Many times cutting back on your game schedule and other referee obligations can be an acceptable option to the painful choice of completely stepping away from the avocation that has given you so much enjoyment.

Charging

Illegal personal contact caused by pushing or moving into an opponent's torso is considered charging.

Players moving with the ball are required to stop or change direction to avoid contact IF the defensive player has obtained a legal guarding position AND is in their path.

Once a defender has gained this legal guarding position, the dribbler must get their head and shoulders past the torso of the defensive player. If contact is made to the defender's torso, it is the fault of the dribbler.

Also, a player with the ball is not permitted to push the torso of the defender to gain an advantage to pass, shoot or dribble. This would be ruled a player-control / charging foul.

Q43: B1 obtains a spot on the court before A1 jumps in the air to catch a pass. Subsequently B1 moves to a new spot while A1 is airborne. A1 lands on one foot and then charges into B1. The official rules a blocking fouls on B1. Is the official correct?

Y   N

Q42 Answer Yes. The double foul is reported and results in no free-throws to be awarded. Play is resumed by using the Point of Interruption (POI) and awarding Team A the ball for a throw-in nearest to the spot where the ball was located when play was interrupted. In this case, it's a designated spot near the division line -- where A2 was dribbling.

Plan

PREGAME

Day / Date:

Location / Level / Tip Time:

Travel Time:

Leave By Time:

My Partner(s):

One thing I will try to do better in today's game is ...

Assess

POSTGAME

What went well today?

Where did we get stuck today?

What will we do different next game?

☐ Pregame Conference Completed

☐ Postgame Review Completed

YOUR PERFORMANCE ASSESSMENT					
Decision Accuracy	1	2	3	4	5
Floor Mechanics	1	2	3	4	5
Game Management	1	2	3	4	5
Rules Knowledge	1	2	3	4	5
Comportment	1	2	3	4	5

$ _____
Fee Amount

☐ Payment Received

Inspire

Fame

"Don't chase love, fame or success. Be the best version of yourself and those things will chase you."

Referees are not washed in the acclaim of rock stars and celebrities, but there is a measure of fame that comes with being ranked near the top of your organization, not matter what the level.

Be careful not to isolate yourself from the rank and file of your association or to spend too much time ingratiating yourself with the coaches. At some point with a game on the line, the cozy coaching relationships inevitably sour, and your only refuge will be to turn to the officials you have chosen to ignore on your way to the top.

Learn

Leaving the Court (Violation)

Players are not permitted to leave the court for an unauthorized reason.

When a player runs off the court to avoid a defender or any unauthorized reasons, these violations should be penalized by the officiating crew. This rule was changed several years ago from a technical foul to a violation to encourage more enforcement and discourage teams from gaining an unfair advantage.

When this violation occurs, the ball is dead and the offended team is awarded a throw-in from the designated spot out-of-bounds nearest to the violation. Additionally, the ball does NOT become dead until a try (or tap) ends or until the airborne shooter returns to the floor, when the violation occurs by an opponent.

Challenge

Q44: A2 and A3 set a double screen near near the endline. A1 intentionally goes out of bounds (leaving the court) in an attempt to run their defender into the screen. The official rules a violation on A1 and awards the ball to Team B for a throw-in. Is the official correct?

Y   N

Q43 Answer No. The official should have ruled a charging foul on A1. Since A1 was in control of the ball, and one foot on the court - time and distance are not a factor for B1 when considering a block vs charge situation. The responsibility is on A1 to avoid contact with the defender. If A1 had NOT touched down on the floor a blocking foul would be appropriately ruled.

Plan

PREGAME

Day / Date:

Location / Level / Tip Time:

Travel Time:

Leave By Time:

My Partner(s):

One thing I will try to do better in today's game is ...

Assess

POSTGAME

What went well today?

Where did we get stuck today?

What will we do different next game?

☐ Pregame Conference Completed

☐ Postgame Review Completed

YOUR PERFORMANCE ASSESSMENT					
Decision Accuracy	1	2	3	4	5
Floor Mechanics	1	2	3	4	5
Game Management	1	2	3	4	5
Rules Knowledge	1	2	3	4	5
Comportment	1	2	3	4	5

$ _____
Fee Amount

☐ Payment Received

Fearless

"I am thankful for all of the people who said NO to me. It's because of them I'm doing it myself."

People are entitled to have a less than favorable opinion of your officiating ability. However, you are under no obligation to embrace that assessment. The watershed moment in your officiating career will be when you begin to FEAR LESS what people think of your skill set, and FEAR LESS about the potential for failure.

This FEAR LESS approach will make your FEARLESS and will drive you headfirst into putting in the 'book and body' work that will make you the best official you can be. And you may just discover that your best is good enough!

Double Personal Foul

A situation in which two opponents commit personal fouls against each other at approximately the same time is considered a Double Personal Foul.

In order to speed up play, when two opponents foul each other at approximately the same time, the game should resume a the point of interruption (POI). No free-throws are awarded for this type of foul. Officials should pay close attention to which team is in-control of the ball when a double personal foul is ruled. This is important since the POI procedure awards the ball back to the team that was in-control when the foul occurred. The ensuing throw-in spot would be designated nearest to where the ball was located and not necessarily where the foul occurred. If a try (or tap) is in flight neither team would be in-control. In this case the alternating-possession procedure (AP arrow) would be used to determine which team is awarded the ensuing throw-in.

Q45: The official bounces the ball to A1 who catches the ball in preparation for a one-and-one free-throw situation. A3 and B3 are subsequently charged with a double personal foul. The officials resume play with the free-throw(s) and lane spaces occupied. Is this correct?

Y   N

Q44 Answer Yes. The official is correct. The violation should be ruled immediately when A1 steps off the court for an unauthorized reason. The ensuing throw-in would be made by Team B a the designated spot nearest to the violation.

Plan

PREGAME

Day / Date: Location / Level / Tip Time:

Travel Time: Leave By Time:

My Partner(s):

One thing I will try to do better in today's game is ...

Assess

POSTGAME

What went well today?

Where did we get stuck today?

What will we do different next game?

☐ Pregame Conference Completed

☐ Postgame Review Completed

YOUR PERFORMANCE ASSESSMENT					
Decision Accuracy	1	2	3	4	5
Floor Mechanics	1	2	3	4	5
Game Management	1	2	3	4	5
Rules Knowledge	1	2	3	4	5
Comportment	1	2	3	4	5

$ _____
Fee Amount

☐ Payment Received

Inspire

Energy

"Be the energy you want to attract."

Take the time to self-scout yourself and examine the type of people you associate with and the type of people you attract.

Do you bring a positive upbeat demeanor into every conversation you take part in? Or are you the person who can find the dark cloud in every silver lining? Like-minded people find comfort in each other's company, so determine if you are in the group huddling under the dark cloud, and if so, make the necessary changes.

Learn

Order of Administration

Penalties for fouls are administered in the order in which the fouls occurred.

When officials rule multiple fouls on players, the fouls are always administered in the order they occurred during the game. If one of the fouls includes a double foul, the point-of-interruption would be the the next foul (penalty) in the sequence. All fouls are reported and recorded properly by the scorer.

When penalties include shooting free-throws at each end of the floor they should be attempted in the order in which the fouls occurred. Treat the last penalty in the sequence as it was the only one that occurred to determine the method of getting the ball back into play. This could be a throw-in or free-throw.

Challenge

Q46: A1 is fouled in the act of shooting by B1. Subsequently A1 shouts derogatory and unsportsmanlike comments toward B1 and is given a technical foul. The officials rule this a double foul and resume play at the point-of-interruption. Are the officials correct?

Y   N

Q45 Answer Yes, this is correct. The POI is A1 attempting a one-and-one free-throw. The double fouls do not result in additional free-throws. If the free-throw try was in flight and missed, the alternating-possession procedure would have been used to determine which team is awarded the throw-in. If the first try was in flight and made, the POI would be the 2nd free-throw.

PREGAME

Day / Date:

Location / Level / Tip Time:

Travel Time:

Leave By Time:

My Partner(s):

One thing I will try to do better in today's game is ...

POSTGAME

What went well today?

Where did we get stuck today?

What will we do different next game?

YOUR PERFORMANCE ASSESSMENT					
Decision Accuracy	1	2	3	4	5
Floor Mechanics	1	2	3	4	5
Game Management	1	2	3	4	5
Rules Knowledge	1	2	3	4	5
Comportment	1	2	3	4	5

☐ Pregame Conference Completed

☐ Postgame Review Completed

$ _____
Fee Amount

☐ Payment Received

Appreciation

"Maybe you have to know the darkness before you can appreciate the light."

The hope is that you won't need an injury or an illness to be jolted into appreciating the Blessing of officiating. Having the mental acuity to process and rule on the fast-paced action taking place in front of you; and the physical ability to get up and down the court to be in a position to manage the game, is a gift.

Officiating the next assigned game, like life itself, is not promised to anyone. The game you have today should be embraced and savored because misfortune could rear its head at any moment and leave you longing for what you had taken for granted.

Hand-Checking

Using hands on an opponent to inhibit their freedom of movement, should be ruled a foul.

A defender who uses their hands on to affect the rhythm, speed, balance and quickness of their opponent, puts the offensive player at a clear disadvantage.

The continual touching or placing of the defender's hands on the ball handler is always considered a foul. A player becomes a ball handler when they receive the ball. This includes a player in the post-position.

Incidental contact while attempting to play the ball would not be considered hand-checking, provided it's not flagrant or intentional.

Q47: A2 receives a pass in the post while being guarded by B2. When A2 receives the ball, B2 continues to maintain an 'arm-bar' on A2's lower back. The official immediately sounds the whistle and rules a hand-checking foul on B2. Is the official correct?

Y   N

Q46 Answer No. These two fouls -- one personal and one technical - did not occur at approximately the same time. The technical foul occurred after the personal foul and were on opponents. The officials should administer the foul penalties in the order in which they occurred by awarding the two free-throws to A1 with lane spaces empty, followed by the technical foul. Team B will be awarded the ball at the division line following the technical foul free-throws.

PREGAME

Day / Date: Location / Level / Tip Time:

Travel Time: Leave By Time:

My Partner(s):

One thing I will try to do better in today's game is ...

POSTGAME

What went well today?

Where did we get stuck today?

What will we do different next game?

YOUR PERFORMANCE ASSESSMENT					
Decision Accuracy	1	2	3	4	5
Floor Mechanics	1	2	3	4	5
Game Management	1	2	3	4	5
Rules Knowledge	1	2	3	4	5
Comportment	1	2	3	4	5

☐ Pregame Conference Completed

☐ Postgame Review Completed

$ _____
Fee Amount

☐ Payment Received

Faith

"Faith is taking the first step even when you can't see the whole staircase."

If you are a new official and your lack of confidence in your ability has delivered a less than stellar start to your career, you need to believe things will get better. Have faith that your hard work in studying the rules and sharpening your mechanics will slow the negative momentum and pivot you towards improvement.

Notwithstanding your individual belief in a higher power, your faith in your ability to formulate a plan for progress; to steadfastly implement the plan; and to learn from your mistakes, will play a critical role in you becoming the official you aspire to be.

Palming (Violation)

Carrying the ball (or palming) occurs when a dribbler allows the ball to come to rest in the their hand.

Palming is a dribbling violation where the player ends one dribble --- then starts another by allowing the ball to come to rest momentarily in their hand. By rule, a player is not permitted to dribble a second time after their first dribble has ended.

When the dribbler turns their hand under the ball, which causes it to rest in that hand, the dribble has technically ended. By continuing the dribble movement after the ball is "palmed" is illegal. Officials should watch for the position of the hand to see if it comes under the ball and if the ball "rests" in the palm during the dribble. The offended team is awarded the ball out-of-bounds for a designated-spot throw-in nearest to the violation.

Q48: While A1 is dribbling, their hand is in contact with the ball with the palm of the hand facing the ceiling. The official rules this a palming violation. Is the official correct?

Y   N

Q47 Answer Yes. The post player A2 is considered a ball handler when receiving the pass. By B2 maintaining the arm-bar on the ball handler, this should be ruled a hand-checking foul. If B2 would have removed their arm/ hand, the official should have ruled the contact incidental as this contact in post play is common, provided neither player gains an advantage.

Plan

PREGAME

Day / Date:

Location / Level / Tip Time:

Travel Time:

Leave By Time:

My Partner(s):

One thing I will try to do better in today's game is …

Assess

POSTGAME

What went well today?

Where did we get stuck today?

What will we do different next game?

☐ Pregame Conference Completed

☐ Postgame Review Completed

YOUR PERFORMANCE ASSESSMENT

Decision Accuracy	1	2	3	4	5
Floor Mechanics	1	2	3	4	5
Game Management	1	2	3	4	5
Rules Knowledge	1	2	3	4	5
Comportment	1	2	3	4	5

$ _____
Fee Amount

☐ Payment Received

Inspire

Knowledge

"Any fool can know. The point is to understand."

Don't be an official who is intimidated by the rulebook or paralyzed by the thought of processing the in-game action in relation to rules written to govern it.

You would be wise to spend time picking the brain of respected officials to get their feedback on the spirit and intent of a rule, particularly those that may have caused a problem for you in a game. There is a difference between knowledge and wisdom, and understanding a rule in its full context will make you a more knowledgeable, and more in-demand, official.

Learn

Fighting

Fighting is a flagrant and combative act that can occur when the ball is dead or live.

There is no place for fighting in the scholastic game of basketball and the penalties are justified as such. Any attempt to strike, punch or kick by using a fist, hands, arms, legs or feet --- regardless of whether contact is made should be penalized as fighting. Additionally attempting to instigate a fight by committing an unsporting act that causes a person to retaliate by fighting, would result in both offenders being penalized. Flagrant fouls are given to participants in a fight and are disqualified from the contest. No free-throws are awarded if a corresponding number of players from each team are involved - otherwise two free-throws are awarded to the offended team for each additional player involved, plus a division-line throw-in.

Challenge

Q49: A1 dunks over B1 and then taunts B1. Player B1 then retaliates and flagrantly kicks A1. The official disqualifies A1 for fighting and awards Team B two free-throws and the ball at the division line to resume play. Is the official correct?

Y   N

Q48 Answer Yes. The dribble has ended when the ball is carried (or palmed) using the dribblers' hand facing skyward. This is a violation.

Plan

PREGAME

Day / Date:

Location / Level / Tip Time:

Travel Time:

Leave By Time:

My Partner(s):

One thing I will try to do better in today's game is ...

Assess

POSTGAME

What went well today?

Where did we get stuck today?

What will we do different next game?

□ Pregame Conference Completed

□ Postgame Review Completed

YOUR PERFORMANCE ASSESSMENT

Decision Accuracy	1	2	3	4	5
Floor Mechanics	1	2	3	4	5
Game Management	1	2	3	4	5
Rules Knowledge	1	2	3	4	5
Comportment	1	2	3	4	5

$ _____

Fee Amount

□ Payment Received

Dream

"A dream isn't something you wake up from; but something that wakes you up."

Have you ever closed your eyes and thought about what you would like your ultimate officiating assignment to be? Is it being on staff in the NBA or WNBA and working a Finals game at this highest level? Or is it being selected as the Referee in a future NCAA championship game?

The competition for these coveted positions is too fierce to think it will happen without a clear vision and a detailed plan to make it happen. Dream, and dream big!

Intentional Foul

Intentional fouls can be personal or technical in nature and may (or may not) be premeditated. These fouls are not based solely on the severity of the act.

Officials should judge whether a player intentionally:

1) Neutralizes an opponent's obvious advantageous position.
2) Contacts an opponent away from the ball, who is clearly not in the play, or not making a play on the ball.
3) Uses contact specifically designed to stop the clock or keep it from starting.
4) Excessive contact while the ball is live (or dead) including an airborne shooter before returning to the floor.
5) Contact with the thrower during a throw-in by reaching through the boundary line.
6) Any contact that cannot be ignored during a dead ball should be considered an intentional technical foul.

The offended team is entitled to two free-throws with no players in marked lane spaces, plus the ball for a throw-in at the nearest spot to the foul.

Q50: Late in the 4th quarter Team B is trailing by 8 points. Team B's head coach begins to yell for his players to "foul quickly" and B1 responds by gently grasping A1 around the waist. The official rules this a common foul as the contact was minimal. Is the official correct?

Y   N

Q49 Answer No. Both A1 and B1 should be charged with flagrant technical fouls for fighting and be disqualified. The actions of A1 taunting which caused B1 to retaliate should be considered a flagrant act. While the actions of A1 alone might not be considered flagrant the resultant fight is a direct outcome of the taunting and should be penalized.

PREGAME

Day / Date: Location / Level / Tip Time:

Travel Time: Leave By Time:

My Partner(s):

One thing I will try to do better in today's game is ...

POSTGAME

What went well today?

Where did we get stuck today?

What will we do different next game?

YOUR PERFORMANCE ASSESSMENT					
Decision Accuracy	1	2	3	4	5
Floor Mechanics	1	2	3	4	5
Game Management	1	2	3	4	5
Rules Knowledge	1	2	3	4	5
Comportment	1	2	3	4	5

☐ Pregame Conference Completed

☐ Postgame Review Completed

$ _____
Fee Amount

☐ Payment Received

Motivation

"Do something today that your future self will thank you for."

An effective visualization exercise is to draw a clear mental picture of what you would like the 'NEW' you to look, act and sound like.

Visualize the NEW you as a respected and in-demand official - thanking the 'OLD' you for making the commitment to change and having the mental and physical discipline to put in the work to make this transformative moment possible.

The 'OLD' you will smile and take pride in the contribution they made to make it all happen.

So get started today to begin shaping the 'NEW' you!

Throw-In

A throw-in is a method of putting the ball in play from out-of-bounds. Besides the throw-in, the free-throw and the jump ball are the only methods of making a dead ball became live.

A throw-in begins and the ball becomes live when the ball is at the disposal of (handed or bounced to) the thrower.

The throw-in count ends when the ball is released by the thrower in a way the passed ball goes directly in the court.

The throw-in ends when the passed ball touches (or is legally touched) by another player inbounds, or out of bounds or the throw-in team commits a throw-in violation.

Q51: Team A is entitled to an alternating-possession throw-in. A1's throw-in pass is illegally kicked by B2. The official awards Team A the ball again while Team A retains the AP arrow. The subsequent throw-in is not considered an AP throw-in. Is the official correct?

Y   N

Q50 Answer No. While many officials might rule this a common foul and argue this is "part of the game." But this is an action by the defender to stop the clock. The lack of severity has no bearing on the "intent" of the defender to gain an unfair advantage. The proper ruling is an intentional foul on B1 with A1 receiving two free-throws and Team A the ball nearest the spot of the foul.

Plan

PREGAME

Day / Date:

Location / Level / Tip Time:

Travel Time:

Leave By Time:

My Partner(s):

One thing I will try to do better in today's game is ...

Assess

POSTGAME

What went well today?

Where did we get stuck today?

What will we do different next game?

YOUR PERFORMANCE ASSESSMENT					
Decision Accuracy	1	2	3	4	5
Floor Mechanics	1	2	3	4	5
Game Management	1	2	3	4	5
Rules Knowledge	1	2	3	4	5
Comportment	1	2	3	4	5

☐ Pregame Conference Completed

☐ Postgame Review Completed

$ _____
Fee Amount

☐ Payment Received

Inspire

Make A Difference

"The purpose of life is not to be happy. It is to be useful, to be honorable, to have it make some difference that you have lived, and lived well."

It is never too early to think about your officiating legacy. By giving some consideration to how you would like to be thought of at the end of your career, this exercise will likely change your present day actions.

Make a conscious effort to give your time and talent to serve your organization in a way that maximizes your abilities and benefits the group (i.e. be an instructor; a fundraising coordinator; run for an elected office, etc.) This selfless mindset will likely improve the quality of your career while undoubtedly enhancing your legacy.

Learn

Screening

A screen is legal action by a player who without causing contact delays or prevents an opponent from reaching a desired position. It is critical screeners establish a legal position prior to incidental contact.

Screeners shall not:
Take a position closer than a normal step from the opponent when they are outside the visual field of a stationary player.
Take a position within their vertical plane with a stance that is wider than shoulder width apart.

When screening a moving player they must allow the opponent time and distance to avoid contact. The speed of the player will determine where the screener may take a position - and may be one or two normal steps from the opponent. If screening an opponent moving in the same path / direction, the player behind is responsible for contact. If the screener violates these provisions and contact occurs, a foul should be ruled.

Challenge

Q52: A1 in attempting to screen a moving B1 and A1 takes a stationary position in B1's path. B1 is aware of A1 and has an opportunity to avoid A1's contact but contact occurs regardless. The official rules a foul on A1 for illegal screening. Is the official correct?

Y   N

Q51 Answer Yes. The violation by Team B during the AP throw-in occurred before the AP throw-in was completed. Team A is awarded the ball for a throw-in and retains the arrow for the next held ball (or end of quarter) situation. This throw-in is not considered part of the alternating-possession procedure. Team A gets possession of the ball and retains the arrow.

Plan

PREGAME

Day / Date:

Location / Level / Tip Time:

Travel Time:

Leave By Time:

My Partner(s):

One thing I will try to do better in today's game is ...

Assess

POSTGAME

What went well today?

Where did we get stuck today?

What will we do different next game?

☐ Pregame
Conference
Completed

☐ Postgame
Review
Completed

YOUR PERFORMANCE ASSESSMENT

Decision Accuracy	1	2	3	4	5
Floor Mechanics	1	2	3	4	5
Game Management	1	2	3	4	5
Rules Knowledge	1	2	3	4	5
Comportment	1	2	3	4	5

$ _____

Fee Amount

☐ Payment Received

Luck

"It is good to be lucky, but I would rather be exact. This way when luck comes along, you'll be ready."

Most successful officials will invariably state that a measure of luck played a part in putting them where they are today. More times than not, it was a series of officiating dominoes that were perfectly aligned and fell at exactly the precise time to create the career they have enjoyed.

But without the knowledge, the poise, the skill and a trained body to execute it all, the lucky dominoes would have fallen like a tree in an empty forest - no one would have heard it.
If and when your luck does arrive; make sure you are ready to put it to good use!

Three Second Violation

A player is not permitted to remain for three seconds (or more) in the restricted lane area while the ball is in control of their team in their own front-court.

This restriction forces offensive players to move without the ball and reduces congestion in the lane area. This restriction also applies to players with one foot touching the lane boundary line. The line is considered part of the lane (except for the lane-space marks).

Players are given an allowance when they have been in the restricted lane area for less than three seconds (in control of the ball) and subsequently dribbles in or moves immediately to try for goal. The violation causes the ball to become dead. The offended team is awarded an out-of-bounds throw-in.

Q53: Player A1 and A2 are in the restricted lane area for 2 seconds when A1 releases a try for goal. A1 get her own rebound and attempts another lay-up and misses. A2 has been in the restricted area for over 4 seconds now. The official ignores this. Is the official correct?

Y   N

Q52 Answer No. This is a legal screen. B1 did not use the opportunity to avoid contact with A1 and is responsible for the contact. B1 is charged with the illegal contact foul as A1 provided proper time and distance when screening a moving player.

PREGAME

Day / Date: Location / Level / Tip Time:

Travel Time: Leave By Time:

My Partner(s):

One thing I will try to do better in today's game is ...

POSTGAME

What went well today?

Where did we get stuck today?

What will we do different next game?

YOUR PERFORMANCE ASSESSMENT					
Decision Accuracy	1	2	3	4	5
Floor Mechanics	1	2	3	4	5
Game Management	1	2	3	4	5
Rules Knowledge	1	2	3	4	5
Comportment	1	2	3	4	5

Pregame Conference Completed

Postgame Review Completed

$ _____
Fee Amount

Payment Received

Modesty

"It is amazing what you can accomplish if you do not care who gets the credit."

You will find that good officiating partners and quality assignments will come to you in abundance if you are an official that is loyal and humble to your referee colleagues. If controversy arises in your game, focus your attention on supporting your partners in order to lift the game above the chaos and get it back on track.

Assignors and supervisors want officials who are confident in their abilities, but who are driven by a desire to deliver high quality game management while remaining in the background. No matter how long you officiate, it is unlikely that anyone will ever pay to see you referee!

Illegal Dribble

Players cannot dribble a second time after their first dribble has ended.

The player is entitled to start another dribble if they lost control of the ball because:

- The opponent touched the ball (and batted it away).
- They attempted a try for field goal.
- They passed (or fumbled) the ball which was subsequently touched by another player.

The penalty includes the ball becoming dead when the violation occurs. The ball is awarded to the opponents for a throw-in at the designated out-of-bounds spot nearest to the illegal dribbling violation.

Q54: Team A's throw-in pass reaches A2 where A2 slaps the ball toward A's front-court. A2 subsequently gains control and dribbles toward the basket. The official rules an illegal dribbling violation. Is the official correct?

Y   N

Q53 Answer Yes. Since there is no team-control during a try for goal, the three second restriction is reset each time Team A rebounds the ball. Provided A2 did not remain in the lane area while her teammate had control of the ball (in their front-court) the official ruled correctly, as this was not a violation.

PREGAME

Plan

Day / Date:

Location / Level / Tip Time:

Travel Time:

Leave By Time:

My Partner(s):

One thing I will try to do better in today's game is ...

POSTGAME

Assess

What went well today?

Where did we get stuck today?

What will we do different next game?

YOUR PERFORMANCE ASSESSMENT					
Decision Accuracy	1	2	3	4	5
Floor Mechanics	1	2	3	4	5
Game Management	1	2	3	4	5
Rules Knowledge	1	2	3	4	5
Comportment	1	2	3	4	5

☐ Pregame Conference Completed

☐ Postgame Review Completed

$ _____
Fee Amount

☐ Payment Received

Fitness

"Being healthy and fit isn't a fad or a trend, it's a lifestyle."

There is a distinct difference between being healthy and being physically fit enough to step onto a basketball court as an official. Being healthy is part Blessing and part lifestyle choices. But avoiding injury and being able to keep up with the fresh young legs every season requires an increasing measure of discipline to watch your weight and stay in good cardiovascular shape.

It is ok to get old; you just shouldn't look, act or run like you are old. Like it or not, perception is reality for many people, so manage the perception you are presenting.

Clock Starts on the Throw-In

One official is always responsible for alerting the timer (by signal) when the clock should be properly started.

If the clock is stopped and play is being resumed by a throw-in, the clock should be started when the ball touches (or is legally touched) by a player on the court, once released by the thrower. The throw-in is now complete. The ball actually is live when it is at the disposal of the thrower. On a designated spot throw-in, this means the ball becomes live first, then the clock starts when the throw-in is completed.

The 5 second count for inbounding the ball is suspended when the thrower releases the ball into the court. The administering official has plenty of responsibilities during a throw-in and needs to be vigilant.

Q55: With 6 seconds left in the game, thrower A1 rolls a designated spot throw-in toward A2. The official continues the 5 second count until the ball is touched by A2, and signals to start the clock. Is the official correct?

Y   N

Q54 Answer No. The dribble does not begin until A1 has gained control of the ball. Slapping the ball does not constitute player-control. This is a legal play.

PREGAME

Day / Date: Location / Level / Tip Time:

Travel Time: Leave By Time:

My Partner(s):

One thing I will try to do better in today's game is ...

POSTGAME

What went well today?

Where did we get stuck today?

What will we do different next game?

☐ Pregame Conference Completed   ☐ Postgame Review Completed

YOUR PERFORMANCE ASSESSMENT					
Decision Accuracy	1	2	3	4	5
Floor Mechanics	1	2	3	4	5
Game Management	1	2	3	4	5
Rules Knowledge	1	2	3	4	5
Comportment	1	2	3	4	5

$ _____
Fee Amount

☐ Payment Received

Value

"Try not to become a person of success. Rather a person of value."

In life, your value doesn't decrease because of another person's inability to see your worth. However with the competitive nature of officiating, your assignor or supervisor has assessed your value and has slotted you accordingly for their purposes. But take great comfort in the fact that your value is a fluid entity and is always being evaluated. This means your officiating fortunes can change in a moment with just one touch of a decision-maker's keyboard.

Quite often creating more availability in your calendar is a great way to increase your value with your assignor. Be sure to exam all ethical options to raise your value with your assignor.

Team Technical Fouls

These types of fouls are not charged directly to any individual, but they do count towards the number of fouls needed for the opponent to reach the one-and-one bonus situation.

When a team technical foul is charged, the offended team is awarded two free-throws plus the ball at the division line for a throw-in. There are many situations where a team is penalized.

They include: Failing to supply rosters and/or starters; adding a player to the roster; changing a number in the scorer's book; identical numbers; illegal communication equipment; failure to occupy the team member's bench as assigned; delay of game; too many players participating in the game; excessive time-outs; unsportsmanlike conduct as a team; crowd unsporting behavior; or failure to return to the court. In addition to these non-contact fouls; a "contact" team technical foul is charged when players lock arms or grasp teammates in an effort to restrict movement of an opponent.

Q56: During a time-out in the 3rd quarter, Team B's coach requests the scorer to add a name to the team list. After several minutes and during the next time-out, Team A's coach notices this infraction and alerts the officials. A team technical foul is issued. Is this correct?

Y   N

Q55 Answer No. The official should suspend the 5-second count when the A1 released (rolled) the ball toward A2. The official was correct in waiting until A2 touched the ball before signalling to start the clock.

PREGAME

Day / Date: Location / Level / Tip Time:

Travel Time: Leave By Time:

My Partner(s):

One thing I will try to do better in today's game is ...

POSTGAME

What went well today?

Where did we get stuck today?

What will we do different next game?

☐ Pregame Conference Completed   ☐ Postgame Review Completed

YOUR PERFORMANCE ASSESSMENT				
Decision Accuracy	1	2	3	4	5
Floor Mechanics	1	2	3	4	5
Game Management	1	2	3	4	5
Rules Knowledge	1	2	3	4	5
Comportment	1	2	3	4	5

$ _____
Fee Amount

☐ Payment Received

Positivity

"The greatness of a person is not in how much wealth they acquire, but in their integrity and ability to affect those around them positively."

At some point in your officiating career, if it lasts more than a few years, it will hit you that you will be remembered more for how you impacted your fellow referees than for the games you will have worked. The secret is to learn and embrace this as early as possible in your career.

Constructive advice will genuinely help others, and also challenge you to practice what you preach, which will make you a better, and more appreciated official. If you demonstrate a consistent selfless spirit to help other officials get what they want, there will be ample opportunities that flow back to you to satisfy your needs.

Traveling Violation

Moving a foot (or feet) in any direction in excess of the prescribed limits when a player is holding the ball is considered a traveling violation.

Some of the prescribed limits are as follows:
- Players who catch the ball with both feet on the floor, may pivot using either foot.
- When one foot is lifted the other is the pivot foot.
- If catching the ball while moving, the player may stop and establish a pivot foot.
- If both feet are off the floor and they land simultaneously on both feet, either foot may be the pivot.
- If landing on one foot followed by the other, the first foot to touch is the pivot foot.
- If landing on one foot, they may jump off that foot and simultaneously land on both feet. This is called a "jump stop" and is legal. In this case, neither foot is permitted to be a pivot foot.

By rule, a player cannot be traveling if they are considered to be legally dribbling.

Q57: A1 catches the ball while both feet are off the floor, lands on the left foot and jumps off that same left foot and subsequently comes to a stop with both feet simultaneously on the floor. A1 lifts the right foot during a try for goal. The official rules this legal. Correct?

Y   N

Q56 Answer No. The actual infraction occurred when the scorer was asked to add (or change) the player in The scorebook. However the foul must be charged when it occurs and enforced when the ball next becomes live. In this case several minutes passed with many live / dead ball situations. It was too late to penalize at this time.

PREGAME

Day / Date: Location / Level / Tip Time:

Travel Time: Leave By Time:

My Partner(s):

One thing I will try to do better in today's game is ...

POSTGAME

What went well today?

Where did we get stuck today?

What will we do different next game?

YOUR PERFORMANCE ASSESSMENT					
Decision Accuracy	1	2	3	4	5
Floor Mechanics	1	2	3	4	5
Game Management	1	2	3	4	5
Rules Knowledge	1	2	3	4	5
Comportment	1	2	3	4	5

☐ Pregame Conference Completed   ☐ Postgame Review Completed

$ _____
Fee Amount

Payment Received

Inspire

Resourceful

"Do what you can. With what you have. Where you are."

The editors of the basketball rulebook could not include in it every 'strange but true' scenario that has ever occurred in a game. You need to know the interpretation and application of the rule pertaining to your out-of-the-blue situation, then bring a genuine sense of fairness and common sense to make your ruling.

If the rulebook does not provide the resource -- that is to say a specific ruling for a clear cut scenario -- then you have to resourceful. Spend time with officials who are considered excellent game managers with a strong streak of common sense.

Learn

Goal

A goal is made when a live ball enters the basket from above and either remains in or passes through the basket.

Whether the clock is running or stopped has no influence on the counting of a goal - provided the ball is live.

No goal can be scored if a throw-in goes untouched through the basket. If a player-control foul occurs before or after a goal the officials should cancel the goal.

After a goal is made, the ball becomes dead, or possibly remains dead, in the case of multiple or technical foul free-throws. If a live ball enters the basket from above and gets "stuck" in the net the goal should be counted.

Challenge

Q58: A1 is attempting a 3 point try from their own backcourt area. The try is short and bounces on the floor and subsequently goes through the basket. The official rules this a 3 point goal. Is the official correct?

Y   N

Q57 Answer Yes, this is a legal play. A1 is permitted to lift either foot after a "jump stop" to pass or attempt a try for goal. A1 would not be permitted to establish another pivot foot in this case. The official ruled correctly even though this play looks strange at full speed.

PREGAME

Day / Date:

Location / Level / Tip Time:

Travel Time:

Leave By Time:

My Partner(s):

One thing I will try to do better in today's game is ...

POSTGAME

What went well today?

Where did we get stuck today?

What will we do different next game?

Pregame
Conference
Completed

Postgame
Review
Completed

YOUR PERFORMANCE ASSESSMENT

Decision Accuracy	1	2	3	4	5
Floor Mechanics	1	2	3	4	5
Game Management	1	2	3	4	5
Rules Knowledge	1	2	3	4	5
Comportment	1	2	3	4	5

$ _____

Fee Amount

Payment Received

Inspire

Nourish

"People are like dirt. They either nourish you and help you grow as a person or they can stunt your growth and make you wilt and die."

If you are entrusted with a teaching position in your officiating organization, be sure to deliver your instruction and critiques with a compassionate spirit.

Feedback from one adult to another that is degrading and mean spirited will almost always miss the mark and any improvement will happen in spite of the message. This doesn't mean that you avoid delivering bad news about an official's prospects for success. Rather, it is about connecting with an official on their shortcomings and offering a clear path for improvement.

Learn

Try

When a player attempts to score two (or three) points by throwing the ball into their team's own basket it should be considered a try.

The try starts when the player begins the motion which precedes the release of the ball. The try ends when one of the following occurs:

- The try is successful.
- The try is determined to be unsuccessful
- When the thrown ball touches the floor.
- When the ball becomes dead.

If a foul occurs by the defense once the try has started, the player should be considered "in the act of shooting" and the ball would remain live, until the try has ended.

Challenge

Q59: A1 gets confused and throws the ball at the wrong basket. A1 is fouled by B1 and the ball goes into the basket. The official disallows the goal. Is the official correct?

Y   N

Q58 Answer No. Two points should be scored. The try for field goal by A1 ended when the ball touched the floor. Sometimes a goal is scored when it's not the direct result of a tap or try. A1 would be credited with two points but not three.

PREGAME

Day / Date: Location / Level / Tip Time:

Travel Time: Leave By Time:

My Partner(s):

One thing I will try to do better in today's game is ...

POSTGAME

What went well today?

Where did we get stuck today?

What will we do different next game?

☐ Pregame Conference Completed   ☐ Postgame Review Completed

YOUR PERFORMANCE ASSESSMENT				
Decision Accuracy	1	2	3	4	5
Floor Mechanics	1	2	3	4	5
Game Management	1	2	3	4	5
Rules Knowledge	1	2	3	4	5
Comportment	1	2	3	4	5

$ _____
Fee Amount

☐ Payment Received

Passion

"Do it with passion or not at all."

If you have made the decision this officiating avocation is worth your energy, as well as your most precious asset - your time - then you owe it to yourself to give it your best effort. Passion can lift you beyond your shortcomings and failures. It will also give you the satisfaction of achievement, along with the peace of mind that comes only from doing all that you can do.

And while experience has its rightful and respected place on the path for career advancement; passion is the one thing that experience can't teach. Passion will report to work ready to go on Day One. Make sure you bring it with you everyday!

Held Ball

The alternating-possession procedure should be used when a held ball occurs.

When two opponents have their hands so firmly on the ball that neither player cannot obtain control without undue roughness, a held ball should be ruled.

When an opponent also places their hand(s) on the ball and prevents an airborne player from throwing the ball, or releasing it on a try, a held ball should be ruled.

A held ball causes the the clock to stop and the ball to become dead. The team that is entitled to the next throw-in via the alternating-possession procedure is awarded the ball for a designated spot throw-in nearest to where the held ball occurred.

Congratulations ... You have completed all the GREAT Official Challenges!

Y   N

Q59 Answer Yes. The ball became dead when the foul occurred, since A1 was not attempting a try at their own basket. When a player throws at the opponent's basket it should not be considered a try for goal. If Team A was in the bonus when fouled they would be awarded a one and one (or two free-throws) at Team A's basket. If not the ball would be awarded to Team A.

Plan

PREGAME

Day / Date: Location / Level / Tip Time:

Travel Time: Leave By Time:

My Partner(s):

One thing I will try to do better in today's game is ...

Assess

POSTGAME

What went well today?

Where did we get stuck today?

What will we do different next game?

YOUR PERFORMANCE ASSESSMENT					
Decision Accuracy	1	2	3	4	5
Floor Mechanics	1	2	3	4	5
Game Management	1	2	3	4	5
Rules Knowledge	1	2	3	4	5
Comportment	1	2	3	4	5

☐ Pregame Conference Completed

☐ Postgame Review Completed

$ _____
Fee Amount

☐ Payment Received

COMPLIMENTARY

Officiating Resources

Weekly In-Season
Newsletters

Expert Articles

Rule Challenges

Discussion Forum

Ref60.com

86733129R00093

Made in the USA
Columbia, SC
05 January 2018